# BOOMERANG

A Kirsty Melville Book

1⊖

Ten Speed Press
Post Office Box 7123
Berkeley, California 94707

Distributed in Canada by Publishers Group West

Design by Liz Nicholson, Design BITE

Library of Congress Cataloging-in-Publication Data:
Jones, Philip, 1955–
    Boomerang: behind an Australian icon / Philip Jones
        p. cm.
    Originally published: Kent Town, S. Aust.:Wakefield Press, 1996.
    Includes bibliographical references.
    ISBN 0-89815-943-1
    1. Boomerangs. I. Title
GN498.B6J65  1997
799.2'028'2—dc21                    97-16261
                                    CIP

Except where indicated, the historical images in this book are reproduced from originals held in the Anthropology Archives, South Australian Museum (AASAM), and the boomerangs and other artifacts illustrated are from the collections of the South Australian Museum.

Artwork for the image used as a background for boomerang photographs is based on an original pental pen drawing by Harry Wintjin, at Indulkana, South Australia, 1980 (AASAM).
The photograph on the half title page is of an Aboriginal stockman ready to throw a boomerang, northern South Australia, ca. 1930 (AASAM).
Cover boomerang A39286, South Australian Museum.

Originally published by Wakefield Press
First Ten Speed Press printing, 1997
Printed in Singapore
1 2 3 4 5 6 7 8 9 10—01 00 99 98 97

# CONTENTS

A boy in northern Western Australia, 1916, carrying an adult boomerang. (H. Basedow; National Museum of Australia)

**An Arrernte man throws a boomerang near Alice Springs, 1926. (AASAM)**

# KARLI

Karliji walya nyampuwardingkinyayirni, yapa nyampu wardingkikirlangu manu nguru nyampuwardingkinyayirni. Yangka kuja kalu nyanyi, ngulaju kalu milya pinyi nguru Australia-wardingki.

Kardiyarlu kalu puta walaparrirni karli nguru nyampauwardingkipiyarlu. Lawajuku kalurla puta warra ngarni karli ngurrgumaninjaku warrakakuju. Kala kuju kalu kardiyarlu manyu pinyi manu kankarlu mani, kula karliji manyuku. Junganyayirni ngurunyampuwardingki.

Kala jalangujalangu yapa kalu nyinami mirninypanyayirni manu rdirrinyapanyayirni karli jarnturnu. Ngulakurlunya kalu yani wirlinyi jalanguju, ngulakurlunya kalunyanu kuluku kuluku mani manu kalu purlapa pinyi manu pirlirrpirlirrpinyi.

Abie Jangala of Lajamanu, 1985

A poster depicting Abie Jangala of Lajamanu with freshly cut wood for *wirlki* or hooked boomerang. Designed by Chips Mackinolty, Jalak Graphics, 1985.

# THE BOOMERANG

The boomerang belongs to this our land which is our true home. When people see the boomerang they recognise it as belonging to the Australian homeland.

White people try, and fail, to copy the boomerang belonging to our own place. Even though they try to make each boomerang exactly the same, not all boomerangs are alike, for example, the *warraka*. The ones the white people make for toys are not the ones we make. This is true for all our people.

But today we still have the knowledge, skill and training of our boomerang makers. This is seen in the way we still use the boomerang for hunting, fighting, ceremonies and music.

Abie Jangala of Lajamanu (in the Tanami Desert), 1985, translation from Warlpiri by Paddy Patrick Jangala

# Localities Mentioned in the Text

## WESTERN AUSTRALIA

1. Forrest River
2. Beagle Bay
3. Derby
4. Moola Bulla
5. Broome
6. Roebuck Bay
7. Balgo
8. La Grange
9. Mandora
10. Port Hedland
11. Roebourne
12. Geraldton
13. Kalgoorlie
14. Perth
15. Albany
16. King George Sound
17. Eucla
18. Fitzroy River
19. Forrest River
20. Ashburton River
21. Lyons River
22. Gascoyne River

## NORTHERN TERRITORY

23. Milingimbi
24. Yirrkala
25. Darwin
26. Pine Creek
27. Daly River
28. Port Keats
29. Katherine
30. Daly Waters
31. Borroloola
32. Tennant Creek
33. Lake Nash
34. Barrow Creek
35. Mount Denison
36. Yuendumu
37. Cockatoo Creek
38. Mt Liebig
39. Hamilton Downs
40. Hermannsburg
41. Alice Springs
42. Tempe Downs
43. Roper River
44. McArthur River

## SOUTH AUSTRALIA

45. Ernabella
46. Oodnadatta
47. Mungeranie
48. Andrewilla
49. Innamincka
50. Coober Pedy
51. Wooltana
52. Mt Serle
53. Nepabunna
54. Mt Chambers
55. Mt Patawerta
56. Myrtle Springs
57. Brachina Gorge
58. Mannum
59. Swan Reach
60. Adelaide
61. Meningie
62. Mount Gambier
63. Murray Bridge
64. Fowlers Bay
65. Yalata
66. Macumba River
67. Warrina Creek
68. Stuart Creek
69. Murray River
70. Cooper Creek

## VICTORIA

71. Ballarat
72. Melbourne
73. Leichardt-Selwyn
74. Gippsland
75. Lake Tyers Mission

## NEW SOUTH WALES

76. Murray River
77. River Darling
78. Mount Browne
79. Sturt's Meadow
80. Broken Hill
81. Sydney
82. Port Stephens
83. La Perouse
84. Broken Bay
85. Farm Cove
86. Port Jackson
87. Canberra

## QUEENSLAND

88. Palmerville
89. Mossman
90. Cairns
91. Kuranda
92. Tully
93. Cardwell
94. Ayr
95. Cloncurry
96. Mitakoodi
97. Hughenden
98. Torrens Creek
99. Landers Creek
100. Kilcummin
101. Winton
102. Alpha
103. Boulia
104. Marion Downs
105. Glenormiston
106. Birdsville
107. Bierbank
108. Noosa
109. Tewantin
110. Brisbane
111. Georgina River
112. Diamantina River
113. Cooper Creek
114. Bulloo River

TORRES STAIT

• Thursday Island

Goulburn
Island

Melville Island

Elcho Island

(25)

(23)

(24)

ARNHEM LAND

(27) (26)

(28)

(29)

(43)

(19) (1)

(30)

KIMBERLEY

(31)

(44)

Groote Eylandt
GULF OF
CARPENTARIA

CAPE YORK
PENINSULA

Mornington
Island

(88)

Bentinck
Island

(89)

(91)

(90)

(2) (3)

(5)

(4)

(6)

N O R T H E R N

(92)

Dunk Island

(93)

GREAT
BARRIER
REEF

(18)

TANAMI DESERT

(94)

Eighty mile beach

(8)

T E R R I T O R Y

(96) (95)

(97) (98) (99)

(9)

(32)

Q U E E N S L A N D

GREAT
SANDY
DESERT

(37)

(33)

(11) (10)

(35)

(34)

PILBARA

(36)

(101)

CANNING STOCK ROUTE

(38)

MACDONNELL RANGES

(105) (103)

(100)

(20)

GIBSON DESERT

(40) (41)

(111)

(104)

(112)

(102)

(21)

(42)

(39)

SIMPSON
DESERT

CANARVON
GORGE

W E S T E R N

(106)

(108)

(45)

(113)

(107)

(109)

(22)

BIRDSVILLE TRACK

(48)

(114)

A U S T R A L I A

S O U T H

(66)

(49)

Lake Killalpaninna

MORETON
BAY

(46)

(47)

(110)

Lake Eyre

(70)

STRZELECKI TRACK

GREAT VICTORIA DESERT

A U S T R A L I A

(50)

(12)

(55) (52)

(53)

(78)

(13)

NULLARBOR PLAIN

(67)

(68)

(51)

(79)

(77)

(65) (64)

(56)

Lake Torrens

(57) (54)

(17)

(80)

N E W   S O U T H   W A L E S

GAWLER
RANGES

FLINDERS
RANGES

(82)

(14)

(69)

Lake Macquarie

(84)

EYRE
PENINSULA

(63)

(59)

(81)

(83)

(85)

YORKE
PENINSULA

(60)

(58)

(76)

(86)

(87)

Lake Albert

(61)

THE
COORONG

V I C T O R I A

(15) (16)

(62)

(71)

(73)

(72)

(74) (75)

T A S M A N I A

# Preface

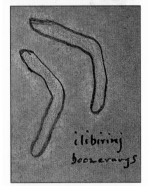

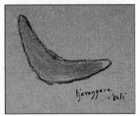

In the European imagination, the boomerang has always expressed a unique quality associated with Australia as a land of paradox. This remarkable object, both a weapon and a toy, which can return to strike its thrower as easily as its target, seems of a kind with the duck-billed platypus, the egg-laying echidna, the bounding kangaroo, or plants which spring into life after bushfires. By concentrating on its eccentric qualities, we have overlooked the central fact about this object – that it represents a remarkable solution devised by Aboriginal people to the difficult challenge of living and prospering in the Australian environment.

Since their arrival in Australia in 1788, Europeans have tended to reduce the many forms, styles and names of Aboriginal boomerangs into a single, inaccurate stereotype. The same process has applied to Aboriginal people themselves, overlooking the great cultural differences which apply across the country.

This book examines the full range of Aboriginal boomerangs encountered by European collectors since the 1860s. Most of the boomerangs illustrated and discussed here are from the collection of the South Australian Museum in Adelaide, which holds the world's largest and most representative collection of Aboriginal artefacts. Many of these boomerangs were obtained on the frontier of contact by missionaries, traders, police, explorers and anthropologists. The individual history of each boomerang takes us back into the particular colonial relationship which framed those encounters. While some evidence confirms that individual boomerangs were stolen, or removed by Europeans in violent circumstances, the great majority of acquisitions were unforced

**Boomerangs drawn by Aboriginal artists across Central and Western Australia during the 1930s and 1950s, annotated by Norman Tindale. His notes show just a few of the hundreds of terms for**

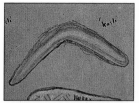

and open. Like European commodities, boomerangs and other artefacts became objects of exchange within a new sphere of contact.

Against this background, perhaps the most direct appropriation of the Aboriginal boomerang has taken place at a symbolic level. The boomerang has been used over and over in the long process of Australian identity formation, taking its place with the world's great cultural symbols. Aboriginal people have also played an active part in this process, of course, and the two histories of the boomerang can no longer be easily separated.

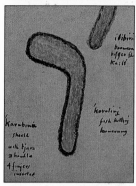

This book has a distinct and unusual pedigree. During 1992 the author and Dr Christopher Anderson (now Director, South Australian Museum) curated a very large exhibition of boomerangs, titled *Boomerang!* The success of this exhibition led to versions of it being displayed in London at the Southbank Centre a year later, and at the San Francisco International Airport during 1996. A suggestion for a Spanish exhibition led ultimately to a new partnership with South Australian Promotions and the funding and production of a completely new product, a CD-ROM titled *Boomerangs: Echoes of Australia.* This is now widely available and features interactive elements such as flight simulations, do-it-yourself boomerang-making kits, as well as a gallery of more than 250 boomerangs from the South Australian Museum collection. This book arises out of all those endeavours.

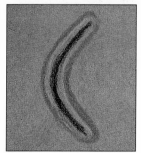

**the boomerang used by speakers of more than 250 Aboriginal languages.** (AASAM)

*Philip Jones, Adelaide, 1996*

# ANTIQUITY

Aboriginal people invented the boomerang thousands of years ago and the circumstances

of that invention will never be known. Perhaps the impetus was

provided by children's games with bent gumleaves placed in the

updraught of a campfire, or by observing the twisting path of a winged

seed, or through concerted experiment by hunters.

Boomerangs from Tutankhamen's tomb, photographed in the Cairo Museum. Until recently, the Egyptian boomerangs found in the tomb of Tutankhamen and other pharaohs were thought to be simple throwing-sticks. It is now believed that at least a few of these may have been return-ing boomerangs. (S. Schrapel)

The idea of imparting aerodynamic qualities to a simple throwing-

stick probably arose independently in several places around the world.

There were immediate advantages, increasing the maximum range of a

throw from about 60 metres (for an ordinary throwing-stick) to about

200 metres (for both non-returning and returning boomerangs).

Archaeologists have dated Ancient Egyptian throwing-sticks, or

hunting boomerangs, to at least 4,000 years ago. The objects also appear in 9,000-year-old rock paintings in North Africa. In 1987 a mammoth tusk carved in the shape of a boomerang was excavated in Poland and has been dated at 23,000 years.

As throwers of non-returning boomerangs, or throwing-sticks, the Australian Aboriginal people were joined by the Hopi Indians in Arizona, the Eskimos, and peoples of India, Indonesia, Vanuatu, Denmark, Holland and Germany, among others. In most of these places the boomerang was apparently made obsolete by the invention of the bow and arrow.

The world's oldest known wooden boomerangs were excavated by the archaeologist Roger Luebbers from a peat bog at Wyrie Swamp in South Australia during 1973. One of those boomerangs is pictured here; its light weight and shape suggest that it was a returning boomerang. (AASAM)

Uncovering boomerang history: Roger Luebbers excavating the Wyrie Swamp boomerangs in 1973. The outline of a boomerang can be seen at his feet. The boomerangs and other wooden artefacts had lain perfectly preserved in a peat swamp for at least 9,000 years. (AASAM)

**International boomerangs (non-returning)**

LEFT:

Egyptian boomerang from the 12th Dynasty (2000–1788 BC). Boomerangs such as this one were used in Ancient Egypt for hunting wildfowl. Egyptian tomb murals show how hunters threw the weapons at flocks of birds as they were flushed from the marshes by trained cats. This boomerang was excavated at Gebelain. A40038

MIDDLE:

This remarkably symmetrical boomerang-shaped throwing-stick was collected in the New Hebrides (Vanuatu) by the Reverend F.G. Bowie in 1919. These non-returning throwing-sticks were used exclusively for sport. A43878

RIGHT:

Hopi Indian rabbit-killing throwing-stick from Northern Arizona, used by the Zuni and Hopi peoples of the south-western United States. This throwing-stick was obtained in 1901 from the Peabody Museum at Harvard. A12051

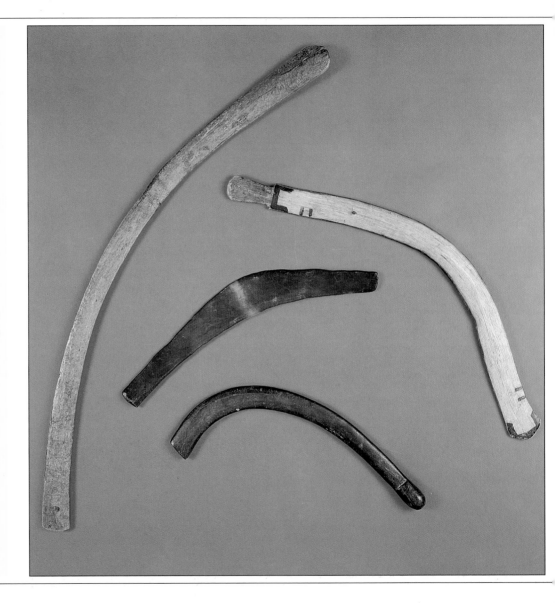

There is no doubt that indigenous Australian people can claim the longest continuous association with the boomerang. The oldest wooden boomerangs known were excavated in 1973 from a peat bog at Wyrie Swamp in the south-east of South Australia. Dated at about 10,000 years, these thin and light boomerangs may have had a returning capacity. Another clue to the boomerang's antiquity in Australia lies in its depiction in the rock art of Arnhem Land – a place where boomerangs have not been used as hunting weapons during the last 9,000 years.

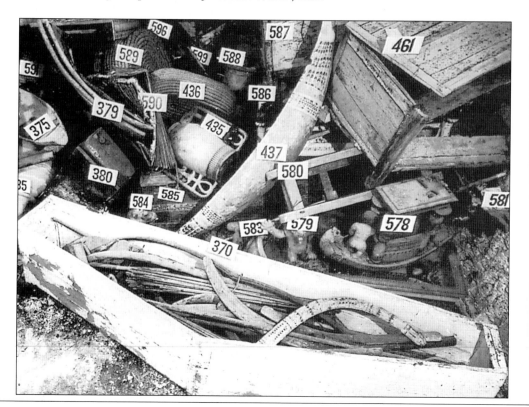

This photograph shows the opened bow-box, containing boomerangs, as discovered by the archaeologist Howard Carter in 1927 in an annexe to the tomb of Egyptian pharaoh, Tutankhamen. (Howard Carter)

# BOOMERANG DREAMINGS

Aboriginal creation accounts describe how the Australian landscape was formed and shaped by Ancestors in the Dreaming. For Aboriginal people this Dreaming period is not remote in time or place but extends into present, living reality. In the Dreaming, many of the features of the land were created by mythological spears, clubs and boomerangs which were hurled into mountains, deserts, rivers and the sea. These founding dramas or Dreamings are re-enacted in Aboriginal song and ceremony, and are represented in rock art, painting and carving.

There is a rich variety of boomerang Dreamings across Australia, reflecting the diversity of Aboriginal language groups.

294. KIRRATINTINI
(Diari Tribe).
To the place of the unfinished
boomerang *karra*. Here the people
of the Mura mura, Pirnawarankana,
once began to make boomerangs,
but only half completed them because they were in a hurry. The
Toa represents a partly finished
boomerang, and the red lands on it
watercourses on the plain.
*REUTHER COLLECTION (152).*

Boomerangs are represented among the small sculpted *toas* which embody the Dreamings of eastern Lake Eyre. This *toa*, Kirratintini, symbolises the boomerang-shaped plain where the followers of the Ancestor Pirnawarankana made boomerangs for themselves but only half finished them.
A6481

Rock art provides enduring evidence that Aboriginal people have used boomerangs in ceremonies for thousands of years. Look closely and you will find several pairs of stencilled boomerangs among the remarkable array of images on this rock wall in Carnarvon Gorge, Queensland. Aboriginal people formed these stencils by blowing a mixture of red ochre and water across the actual artefacts, leaving behind a negative image. The fact that the boomerangs are depicted in pairs is significant, as boomerangs are often used in pairs in ceremonies and music-making. (Grahame Walsh)

Not surprisingly, it is usually the *returning* boomerang which features in Aboriginal Dreamings. The stories refer to the magic of flight itself, as well as the mystery of an object which flies out of sight and then returns . . .

# Purlka-purlkakurlu

This boomerang Dreaming was painted in 1983 by Paddy Japaljarri Sims, a Warlpiri man, as one of the series of Yuendumu School Doors, now part of the South Australian Museum collection. The English translation of his explanation of this painting was published in a book of the Doors paintings (Warlukurlangu Artists 1992):

*The Old Men carved their boomerangs in preparation for battle. They were Dreamtime Men and they sat carving boomerangs so that they could go and attack other Old Men. The Old Men went and chopped down a tree. They brought the roughly hewn piece of wood back home to carve it into fine boomerangs. They made a great number of these big splendid boomerangs. First they tried out one boomerang. It flew through the air, turned around and came back to them.*

*'It's a good one! This is a good boomerang which has come back true.'*

*It was an excellent boomerang which flew through the air, went right around and came back to the person who had thrown it. They threw another small one. It spun around and came back to its owner. They were ready to do battle and so they tested out their boomerangs.*

*'I'll throw this one well. Right on target. It's a good, accurate boomerang.'*

*Indeed, it flew through the air, swept around and came back to the starting point. All the Old Men watched it.*

*Then the fight started. They went after each other with axes. They went a long way*

# Old Men Dreaming

*south. At the place where they started fighting there are now rocky hills. They threw boomerangs at each other; they fought with axes and boomerangs.*

*After having fought with the axes they buried them in the ground. At the place where they buried them there is now a big rockhole. There are many rockholes there, formed from those axes which the old Dreamtime Men buried at that place. There is also a high sandhill which is called Kankarlarra. There is water there. The weapons of the Dreaming turned into Desert oaks which now grow in that sandhill country.*

*The Dreamtime Men who fought at that place were Japaljarris and Japangardis. Those Old Men turned into birds – falcons and kites.*

*This is a true story of what happened in the Dreamtime. The story belongs to me and I have painted it here.*

*The axes which those Old Men made were all wrong: they were crooked and bent. And when they made the boomerangs they threw one which travelled to another place where it fell down and became a soakage. It travelled a long way.*

*When the Old Men gathered to fight each other, they stormed forward in ranks and they were very big men who had difficulty running. They swayed from side to side. All the young men sat and watched the Old Men fight each other.*

*'Oh, look at those poor Old Men. They are hurling boomerangs at each other'.*

*The Old Men hit each other with boomerangs, and as they were struck they turned into birds and flew away into the air – they turned into all sorts of birds like falcons, kites, hawks. They are the birds which still fly in our skies today.* (Paddy Japaljarri Sims, Warlukurlangu Artists 1992: 31)

ABOVE:

1. *warna* (snake)
2. *warnirri* (waterhole)
3. *wiinywiinypakurlangu wirliya* (falcon's track)
4. *kurrupurda* (boomerang)
5. *watiya* (wood)
6. *warlkurru* (axe)
7. *wirlki* (boomerang)

# Yuduyudulya and the Left-handed Boomerang

This image of a Flinders Ranges rock engraving depicts the central figure of a hunter or warrior with four boomerangs. In a Ngadjuri Dreaming, the ancestral lizard Kudnu restored the sun to a darkened land by throwing a returning boomerang to the north, west, south, and finally, the east. The association of the lizard in this engraving (at left) with boomerangs may possibly relate to this Dreaming.

These motifs date from an earlier period of Aboriginal occupation in the Ranges, perhaps more than 10,000 years ago. (Mountford & Edwards 1964)

This boomerang Dreaming from the Flinders Ranges was told to linguist Dorothy Tunbridge by Adnyamathanha elder Annie Coulthard.

*A long time ago Yuduyudulya the blue wren set out to go from Manggunanha to Marlawadinha Spring. Manggunanha is a hollow, and Yuduyudulya went into the ground there, and came out on the ridge of a low hill just north of Mount Chambers and Marlawadinha. He went along the ridge for a little way. You can see where he went by the line of broken white quartz along the hill. This quartz is actually the feathers which Yuduyudulya dropped as he went along.*

*Standing on the ridge and facing the mountain, with his left hand Yuduyudulya threw a comeback boomerang at the eastern end of the rock wall. There is a heap of white quartz at the spot from which he threw the boomerang. The boomerang broke into pieces. It is now rock spilling down the mountain under the cut it made.*

*Yuduyudulya then ran further along the ridge [towards the west] and threw another comeback boomerang towards the rock face. This boomerang went right through the mountain making a big gap in it. It went on southward, and Yuduyudulya waited for it to turn around and come back to him. It spun around towards the west, but on the way back it hit the top of the western end of the mountain and stopped there. The boomerang is still there. You can see it sitting up on top of Wadna Yaldha Vambata.* (Tunbridge 1988: 120)

# Boomerang Dreamings from the Lake Eyre Region

The eastern Lake Eyre landscape is peppered with Aboriginal sites with mythological boomerang associations. For example, the deep waterhole at Kirrawirina (*kirra* = boomerang) was formed when the Ancestor Mardumana threw his returning boomerang 60 kilometres, from Killalpaninna to Kudnangaua (Kanowana). He used such force that it came back and bored its way into the ground. Another Ancestor, Pirnawarankana, named a waterhole Kirramandra to commemorate the boomerang which he had made. The boomerang returned to him when he tested it, which pleased him so much that he named the place after it.

The Swan History or Dreaming site at Lake Gregory, north of the Flinders Ranges, is also associated with a mythological boomerang. This History describes how the ancestors of the eastern Lake Eyre people obtained fire in the Dreaming. At that time, these human ancestors had fire until it was stolen from them by Simpson Desert people. One of the ancestors, Watapijiri, then turned into a black swan and flew south in search of fire. When she reached Lake Gregory she discovered an old woman, Ngardutjelpani, who had a fire-stick. The two women fought over the fire-stick. Watapijiri threw a boomerang at Ngardutjelpani and after falling to the ground it became a curved peninsula in the lake, known to Aboriginal people in historic times as a favourite place for gathering swan eggs. During the struggle Watapijiri snatched away the fire-stick and flew away with it in her beak. The red beak of the black swan thus had a particular significance for the eastern Lake Eyre people. (Jones & Sutton 1986: 68; 86; 98; 121).

These small carved *toas* depict Aboriginal Dreaming sites of the eastern Lake Eyre region. The *toa* second from left depicts a hill called Ngarakalina; the others refer to sites where Dreaming Ancestors made or used boomerangs. (Jones & Sutton 1986)

Front and back views of a pair of boomerangs used as clapsticks in the Ngapa or Water Dreaming Ceremony, one of the principal Dreamings passing through Warlpiri country, north-west of Alice Springs. When a particular ceremony is performed, individuals belonging to the social classes or 'skin' groups with rights in the Dreaming ensure that the appropriate designs are painted properly.

Charlie Tarawa Tjungurrayi made and painted these boomerangs in 1976. As he made them especially for the ceremony, they lack the usual fluted carving found on hunting boomerangs. During the late 1970s Aboriginal men of the Western Desert communities experimented with acrylic paints, beginning a new and exciting painting movement. These boomerangs were collected by Richard Kimber at Browns Bore, Northern Territory. Top: 600 mm, A67068 Bottom: 680 mm, A67069.

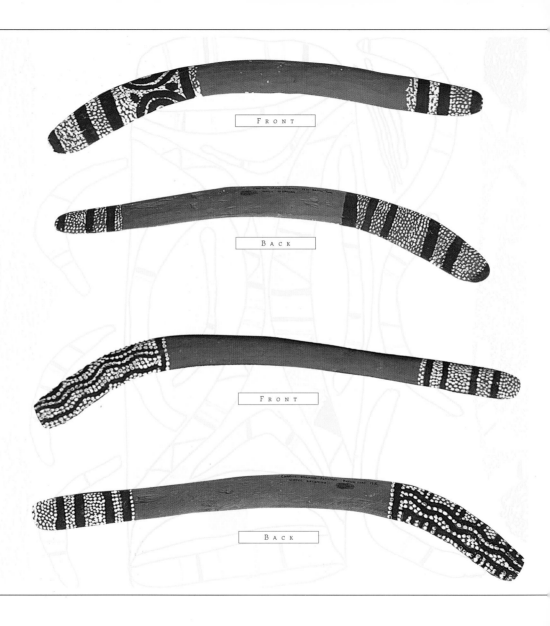

FRONT

BACK

FRONT

BACK

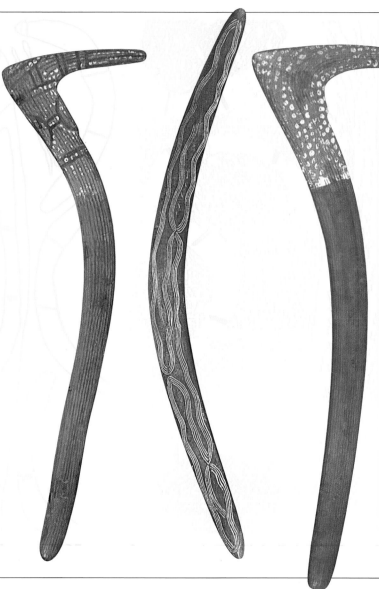

The elaborate painted designs on this hooked boomerang indicate its ceremonial function. The boomerang's irregular form suggests that it may have been made locally, rather than traded north from the usual source of these hooked boomerangs. This example was collected during the early 1890s by police-inspector Paul Foelsche at Daly Waters in the Northern Territory. 690 mm. A5461

MIDDLE:

The fine carvings on this boomerang may indicate the path of a Dreaming ancestor. The station overseer and storekeeper G.H. Birt collected the boomerang from Aboriginal people of the Paroo River in north-western New South Wales during the 1890s. The carvings were probably added with an animal tooth engraver, then filled with gypsum or pipeclay to highlight the effect. 700 mm. A5576

RIGHT:

In its simple, red-ochred form, this hooked boomerang, or *wirlki*, was an ordinary hunting or fighting weapon. By adding painted decorations, the boomerang's owner has transformed its function. Against the characteristic panel of white dots the faint outline of a black design can be seen. These black designs usually consisted of a motif representing the owner's Dreaming. After the completion of ceremonies the owner or performer smudges these black designs, marking the transition back to the secular world. This boomerang, once in the collection of Adelaide's Lord Mayor, Charles Glover, was originally collected from Kaytej or Warlpiri people in the Northern Territory by Charles Chewings, an explorer and prospector. 810 mm. A61639

# MAKING BOOMERANGS

Aboriginal boomerang-makers can instantly recognise the shape of a potential boomerang in a tree, ready to be cut out.

The photograph on this page shows the stages as a piece of mulga wood becomes a finished north-central Australian hooked boomerang (*wirlki*). These boomerangs are usually made from the junction between a mulga tree root and trunk, as this gives maximum strength to the hook. Red ochre, mixed with fat or grease, is added to preserve the boomerang and make it 'strong'.

A58342–6

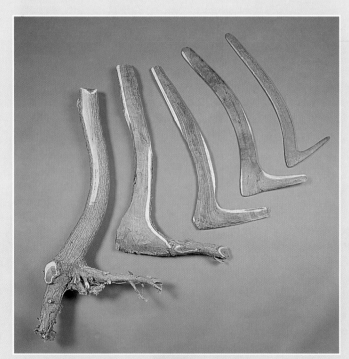

# Types of Timber

Aboriginal people have used a great range of hardwood timbers from across Australia to make boomerangs. In the Centre, the favoured wood is mulga (*Acacia aneura*), or 'dead finish' (*Acacia tetragonophylla*). The hooked boomerangs of north-central Australia derive their shape and strength from the junction of a root and trunk of these strong acacia trees. To the east of the Simpson Desert, where boomerangs are no longer used in daily life, the gidgea (*Acacia georginae*) was favoured.

In the coastal regions of eastern and western Australia boomerang-makers relied on the wood of the mangrove tree. Further inland, in south-eastern Australia, the sheoak or casuarina was preferred. This is an excellent timber for making returning boomerangs as its rippled grain allows a sharp angle without loss of strength.

Artetye apele arne atningke anthurre-arle lyapeme. Arne nhenhe ikwere-ntyele arelhe tyerrtyele ilye, alkwerte, urrempere arlke mpwareme.

*The mulga tree grows all over the place. From this tree Aboriginal people make boomerangs, shields, and shovel spears.*

(Eastern and Central Arrernte text, Henderson & Dobson 1994: 108).

The curve in this mulga trunk is perfect for making two boomerangs. Jack Jakamara Ross, a Warlpiri elder, contemplates the next stage at Cockatoo Creek in 1996. (P. Jones)

Two key traditional implements used in making Central Australian boomerangs: a stone axe dating from the 1880s, and a woodworking adze with stone tools mounted at each end, dating from the 1930s. A41977, A34046.

OPPOSITE PAGE:

This photograph, taken near Alice Springs in the 1930s, shows an Arrernte man carving fluted grooves onto a hunting boomerang. He is using a metal engraving tool mounted on a wooden adze. Metal tools quickly replaced stone artefacts following European contact in Central Australia. (R. Battarbee, AASAM)

# Traditional Tools

Across Aboriginal Australia, the carving of boomerangs and many other wooden objects was solely men's work. This situation has altered during the past hundred years, so that women play a major role in woodcarving today.

Before the advent of metal tools men cut boomerangs using stone axes and adzes. Adzes consisted of a stone blade mounted in resin at the end of a slightly bowed length of wood about 60 centimetres long. In eastern Central Australia a sharper engraving flint was sometimes mounted at the other end.

Finishing tools were usually stone scrapers, but shell scrapers or 'spokeshaves' have been recorded from south-eastern Australia.

Appropriate stone tools were treasured items. The particular stone for their manufacture often passed through trade networks from distant quarry sites.

Alywekele artwele panthe, alye-arlke mpwareke arrwekele, lyete aneme itne *crowbar*-le mpwareme, *screwdriver*-le-arle itne mpwareme.

*Before, men used to make large coolamons and boomerangs with stone tools, but nowadays they make them with screwdrivers or the sharpened leaf of metal from a car's springs.*

(Eastern and Central Arrernte text, Henderson & Dobson 1994: 109).

# Carving the Boomerang

Aboriginal men of eastern Lake Eyre were adept in the use of a stone adze in carving and finishing their boomerangs. To the west of Lake Eyre these adzes were mounted on the handle of spearthrowers.

Here a Wangkangurru man shows how boomerangs were made, using his feet as a vice to steady the wood, and making controlled strokes with the adze.

Before Europeans brought metal to Australia, Aboriginal men split blocks of wood from trees with stone axes and wooden wedges. Depending on its thickness, a block could be split to produce a pair of boomerangs. The maker then worked the split wood with a stone chisel to produce the boomerang's rough shape. This close and careful work was undertaken by one man, using his feet and legs as a vice to keep the wood steady, while working the adze towards his body.

Once adzed to a suitable dimension, he finished shaping the boomerang with a hand-held scraper or a shell 'spokeshave'. He smoothed the surface with a fine-grained grinding stone and added incised decoration with a stone, kangaroo or possum-tooth engraver.

In 1897 ethnographer Walter Roth described methods Aboriginal carvers used to cure the wood, steaming and bending it:

*The weapon is originally cut out from the side of a tree-trunk en bloc, then gradually got into shape with a chisel etc, and finally smoothed off with a piece of sharp-edged flint or glass. With wood of suitable grain, white-gum for example, the original block may be split down and two boomerangs made of it. Any defect in shape, in the nature of a bend or twist, can be remedied by various artificial means . . . The Aboriginals throughout all the different ethnographical districts both know and practise various methods of bending or straightening timber, either when already cut or in the rough. Thus, a dry heat in ordinary sand, a moist heat from burning freshly-gathered gum-leaves, or moisture in general, such as soaking in water, is employed for bending any of their wooden implements into shape as required. In order to maintain and preserve the timber in the position attained by one or other of the preceding processes, the whole is covered thickly with grease and fat, saurian or mammalian.*

*The mode of manufacture of the hooked variety varies somewhat from the preceding, the portion of trunk for its shaft being cut out at the same time with an adjacent branch or rootlet for its hook.* (Roth 1897: 142; 102; 142)

George Aiston, amateur ethnographer, retired policeman and Birdsville Track storekeeper, was one of a small group of Europeans who carefully observed the entire process of boomerang manufacture. He noticed a detail often overlooked by other commentators – the care which Aboriginal craftsmen took to ensure that their boomerangs were well seasoned. His letter to a friend and fellow collector, W.H. Gill, written on 14 January 1939, also contains an interesting observation about the average lifespan of an ordinary hunting boomerang:

*The [men] never seasoned their weapons to keep – they only last at most a few weeks, usually they were broken in the first week. The wood was cut green and placed in water or wet sand, until it was shaped and smoothed, then it was put in hot ashes to steam out the water, and when no more water oozed out it was thoroughly greased, then put in the ashes again to melt in the grease, finally it was smeared with fat and red ochre.*

(Aiston to Gill correspondence, Mitchell Library, Sydney)

His grandson watches on as he adzes the surface and smoothes the surface with a grinding stone. Photographed in about 1920 by the Birdsville Track police-trooper and ethnographer, George Aiston (G. Aiston, AASAM)

ABOVE (ALSO SEE PHOTOGRAPH ON PAGE 19): **Jack Jakamara Ross carves out the rough shape with a hand axe, then uses a traditional adze with a metal blade to refine the shape, before heating the boomerang on the fire and levering it straight.** (P. Jones)

After European contact, Aboriginal carvers instantly preferred metal axes and chisels. Glass scrapers became the favoured finishing tool. In the short term, this led to finer work, and possibly even an increase in the manufacture of artefacts. As the European demand for boomerangs increased with the advent of the tourist trade during the 1930s, there was a tendency to produce cruder and less well-balanced boomerangs for sale. Carvers often paid more attention to the designs engraved on boomerangs than to their balance and flight.

Despite this, many Aboriginal carvers across Australia retain and practise their traditional skills, as shown here by Henry Hunter and Jack Jakamara Ross.

European Australians began manufacturing boomerangs for sale during the 1930s and by the 1950s plastic had begun to replace wood as the dominant material. Today it is possible to buy a boomerang made in America from laminated Finnish birch, or from completely artificial materials, such as phenolic resin composite.

BELOW:

Henry Hunter, Baadi man, making a set of boomerangs. Dampier Pensinula, Western Australia, 1996 (W.Barker)

The design on this Cooper Creek hunting boomerang has been achieved by carving fine, parallel lines across the surface, resulting in a fluid, symmetrical pattern. The incisions, probably carved with a wallaby tooth graver, have been highlighted with white pipeclay. This substance, prepared from a mixture of hydrated gypsum and water, was also used for body-painting. 780 mm. A5572

ABOVE:

A possum tooth engraver used for engraving designs on wooden objects including boomerangs, collected by the missionary Oskar Liebler at Hermannsburg, Northern Territory, between 1910 and 1913. A1299

# Designs and Decoration

It seems that very few Aboriginal designs were intended purely for decorative purposes in pre-European times. Traditional painted designs or carvings found on boomerangs across Australia usually refer to Dreaming Ancestors and to local territory associated with these Dreamings.

The geometric carvings of the Kimberley, the looped inscriptions of the Darling River, or the cross-hatched chevron shapes of south-western Queensland all have these associations. The fluted carving on the classic Central Australian boomerangs has no symbolic meaning, but these boomerangs are often decorated for ceremony by painting one end with a panel of dots or shapes with Dreaming associations.

Boomerangs have been incorporated into art by Aboriginal people for thousands of years – examples can be seen in the rock carvings of the Pilbara and the Sydney–Hawkesbury region, or in the rock paintings of Arnhem Land (where hunting boomerangs were apparently not known in recent centuries). Boomerangs now form an important element of contemporary Aboriginal art, serving as 'canvases' for individual artistic expression, decorated with acrylic paints and a range of contemporary motifs.

Pioneering anthropologists W.B. Spencer and F.J. Gillen gave this account of the traditional methods used to apply painted designs of black lines and white dots to a Central Australian boomerang:

The black is simply charcoal mixed with grease, and is applied first, the tip of the finger being usually dipped into the pigment and used as a brush. After that a short twig is taken, the end of which is about the same diameter as it is desired to make the dots. First of all it is cut off square, and then frayed out with the teeth so as to form a brush. The pipeclay is most usually moistened in the mouth. It is a somewhat curious scene to watch a number of natives chewing the pipeclay, which has been previously roughly powdered . . . and then spitting the semi-fluid material out into a pitchi or receptacle of some kind. One would think that the grit would be very objectionable, and that it would be much simpler and more pleasant to grind it down and mix it with water on a stone; but though this is sometimes done, it is more usual, when preparing material for ceremonies, first of all to grind the pipeclay until such time as it has the consistency of coarse sand, and then to chew it in the mouth. When all is ready, the twig-brush is dipped into the white paste, and then simply dabbed down onto the surface of the object being decorated, on which it forms a white disc of the same size as the end of the brush. It is a very simple and effective way of producing a white disc . . . the lines and dots have no definite relation to the original longitudinal flutings, being arranged quite independently of the direction in which they run. (Spencer and Gillen 1927: 559)

Made in 1965 by a Ngalea man at Yalata for the emerging tourist market, this boomerang is slightly broader than a traditional hunting boomerang. The reason for this was probably to accommodate the carved designs, etched in pipeclay. These designs tell the story of a man and his dog, tracking a bush turkey and a kangaroo from waterhole to waterhole (shown as circles) on the Nullarbor Plain. 590 mm. A55808

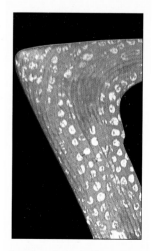

A section of a hooked boomerang decorated in the way described by Spencer and Gillen. (A61639)

FRONT

BACK

**ABOVE:**

This boomerang displays a remarkably complex coiled design, suggesting animal tracks and the path taken by a hunter. It was collected during the 1890s on the Paroo River in south-western Queensland by the station overseer G.H. Birt. 800 mm. A5588

**BELOW:**

This boomerang is likely to have been a fighting weapon decorated with the maker's totemic designs. In this case, the designs appear to represent boomerangs. This example was collected by Queensland meteorologist Clement Wragge from Torrens Creek, east of Hughenden, during the 1890s. 550 mm. A5615

TOP (THIS PAGE):

A boomerang made for the centenary of Victoria's foundation as a colony. The allegorical scene depicts an Aboriginal camp, with a hunter standing before a bridge, looking across to the outline of a city in the distance. This example indicates that the Flinders Ranges carving technique, involving finely-incised carving around blank designs, had also reached into Victoria by the 1930s. 400 mm. A69585

BOTTOM:

One of the finest examples of post-European Aboriginal woodcarving, this boomerang depicts the conflict that occurred between Europeans and Aboriginal people in the Flinders Ranges, particularly during the 1850s and 1860s. The technique of leaving the blank figures to stand out in relief against a pecked background of incisions was also used in the Gawler Ranges. The figures were sometimes soaked in water so that they swelled out, then singed black for effect. 530 mm. A61412

FRONT

BACK

MIDDLE:

Typical in form of Kimberley boomerangs, with an open shape and pointed ends, this boomerang features some remarkable carving, infilled with white pipeclay over an ochred surface. The convex side features the 'greek key' or 'interlocking key' design characteristic of traditional carving in the region (but note the emu design on the left wing). The other, flat side features figurative carving as found in rock art of the region. The large, four-footed animal may represent a bullock. This boomerang was collected during the 1890s at Broome. 540 mm. A21348

# HOW BOOMERANGS FLY

When you throw an ordinary stick, even with tremendous force, it will obey Newton's law of physics, as will a spear, an arrow, or a bullet. Its predictable path is governed by the same formula: distance = time x velocity.

When you throw a returning boomerang, no such predictability applies. The returning boomerang shares its aeronautical principles with a flying discus, a banking airplane, a propeller, a helicopter and a gyroscope. Few mechanical inventions display so many scientific laws. These include Bernoulli's Principle of differential air pressure, gyroscopic stability and gyroscopic precession, and Newton's laws of motion.

A returning boomerang is always thrown in the vertical plane, usually at a 45 degree angle to the thrower. It leaves the thrower's hand, spinning up to ten revolutions a second and travelling at speeds of up to 100 kilometres per hour. Gravity causes the boomerang to tip over into the horizontal plane, taking on the characteristics of a discus.

This night time exposure of an illuminated boomerang's flight shows an elliptical path of 120 metres out and back to the invisible thrower. (E.Darnell)

As the arms spin around, the leading edge presents an airfoil profile. The air must travel over this profile, up over the upper convex surface, as well as across the lower, flat surface. Bernoulli's Principle dictates that both parcels of air must arrive on the other side of the airfoil or wing at the same time. For this to happen, the upper parcel, which is negotiating a longer distance over the upper convex surface, must travel faster. In doing so, it exerts less downward pressure and the result is that the boomerang tends to lift, while still moving forward, away from the thrower.

**AIRFLOW**

Lower Pressure

Higher Pressure

**DIFFERENTIAL PRESSURE**

Lift

**RESULT–LIFT!**

Drag on the wings causes the boomerang's rotation to slow, and as it does so, another force takes effect, that of gyroscopic precession. The unequal air speeds of the two rotating arms (the leading arm is followed by a trailing arm) cause the boomerang to veer to one side, so that it begins to turn in an arc, back towards the thrower. The boomerang (still rotating up to ten times each second) acts as a gyroscope, so that the force to one side is translated not into a direct movement in that direction, but into a 'precessing' movement. That is, the boomerang rotates gradually around a vertical axis as it continues to move through the air, back to the thrower.

This seems complex enough, but the latest research suggests that the non-returning boomerang embodies even more sophisticated principles. For example, the fluted longitudinal carvings on a Central Australian hunting boomerang may achieve an effect similar to the dimples on a golf-ball by reducing the surface tension and air-drag as it flies through the air.

The boomerang is still being studied and analysed more than two centuries after its discovery by Europeans and is still not completely understood. Measured against the millennia of use by its Aboriginal inventors, this is hardly surprising.

Thomas Worsnop, collector and nineteenth-century ethnographer, was one of a number of Europeans to express wonder at the Aboriginal mastery of the returning boomerang: *The throwing of this weapon is an art which few, if any, Europeans can attain to. In the hands of [Aboriginals], however, it is thrown with ease. It at once attains a rapid rotatory motion and ascends to a good height, occasionally taking opposite directions or forming a circle in the air, returning to the thrower, who has to keep a watchful eye so that he is not struck by it, for should it do so it would either inflict a severe wound or, if it struck a vital part, would most certainly kill him. The distance to which it can be thrown is about 100 yds or 150 yds; and in returning it may strike the ground some 20 yds or 25 yds behind the thrower, skimming along the surface for some distance. Sometimes the boomerang is thrown at a point on the ground about 20 ft. or 30 ft. in front, which having struck, it ascends with the usual gyrating motion, returning again in the usual manner . . .*

*When a skilful thrower takes up a boomerang intending to throw it he carefully examines it (even if it be his own manufacture), and holding it in his hand by one end, he moves slowly from side to side, looking intently at the object he purposes striking with it, most carefully noticing the direction and force of the wind, as shown by the moving leaves of trees and the waving of the grass; and not until he has got into the right position will he shake the weapon slightly so as to feel his muscles are under command. More than once he will make an effort as if to throw it, until at the last moment, when he feels he can strike the wind at the right angle, all his force is thrown into the effort, and the missile leaves his hand in a direction nearly perpendicular to the surface. The right impulse has been given, and it quickly turns its flat surface to the earth, gyrates on its axis, rising in the air at the same time, makes a wide sweep, and returns with a quivering or fluttering motion to the thrower.* (Worsnop 1897: 129-130)

**Three diagrams of boomerang flights witnessed during the 1890s near Grafton, New South Wales. The same Aboriginal man made each throw consecutively, with perfect control. On the third throw, the boomerang clipped the ground before returning to the thrower.** (Jennings & Hardy 1899)

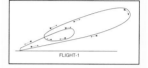

FLIGHT-1

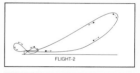

FLIGHT-2

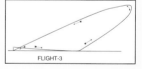

FLIGHT-3

# THE MANY USES OF THE BOOMERANG

In the arid centre of Australia, where survival often depended on the mobility of a group relying on the bare minimum of material possessions, Aboriginal people used a single object for a variety of functions.

**Warlpiri men digging for bush onions with boomerangs on the banks of Cockatoo Creek, near Yuendumu, 1931.** (T. Harvey Johnston)

The Central Australian hunting boomerang is a prime example. It eliminated the need to carry a number of different tools. It was used as a knife, a hammer or club, a digging tool, for making fire by friction, for musical accompaniment as a percussion instrument – as well as its main function as a hunting or fighting weapon.

In more temperate areas, towards the coast and along river systems, mobility was not such a pressing need, and people used different

As an all-purpose tool and weapon, the Central Australian boomerang was always within reach. These three Warlpiri men are eating the bush onions (*yelka*) they have dug out with their boomerangs. (H.J. Wilkinson, AASAM)

artefacts for specialised functions. They used non-returning boomerangs as hunting and fighting weapons, and used returning boomerangs in hunting wildfowl in the coastal greenbelts of south-eastern Australia and Western Australia. Returning boomerangs were also used in games and competitions.

Beyond their obvious utilitarian functions, Aboriginal boomerangs often serve as objects of social and religious significance. Their important role in trading relationships underlines this, as does their association with Dreaming Ancestors, believed to have shaped the landscape as it is today.

# Fighting Boomerangs

Europeans in Australia have often been confused as to the difference between returning boomerangs and boomerangs used for fighting or for hunting game. The fact is that most boomerangs did not come back – most hunting and fighting boomerangs were thrown to hit their targets, not to return.

Thrown at a range of 100 metres or less, the different forms of medium-weight throwing boomerangs used across Australia were all capable of inflicting death or serious injury. This was particularly the case if they were sharpened and spinning fast at contact. Ricocheted off the ground towards an enemy, the swerving flight of these boomerangs was almost impossible to avoid. The hooked boomerangs of northern Central Australia were also potentially lethal – the hook would catch on a parrying shield or club, causing the boomerang to swing around and strike the defender.

Most Australian boomerangs were non-returning, and a large number were never thrown. This applies to the long and heavy boomerangs used across a wide area of eastern Central Australia. Examples in the South Australian Museum measure up to two metres. These *murrawirri* boomerangs were formidable fighting weapons, used in hand-to-hand combat after smaller boomerangs and clubs had been thrown. Combatants exchanged blows and blocked each other's moves. Women also occasionally used the *murrawirri*, which were left in camp when men went hunting.

The following text is in the Eastern and Central Arrernte languages:

Ilye irlpakerte nhenhe ulkere arne artwekenhe. Artwele ilye nhenhe ulkere renje atwerretyeke atnyenewarretyarte, kere aherre apeke irrtyarte tnyante nternetye-akkenhele ilye irlpakerte nhenhe ikwerele ulkere anteme tnyante atwerne irrtyarte iperre itethe akwete anerlenge.

*The number seven boomerang is a weapon that belongs to men. They used to keep them to fight with, or for finishing off kangaroos if they're still alive after spearing them.*

(Henderson & Dobson 1994: 108)

The missionary and linguist Lancelot Threlkeld worked among the Aboriginal people of Lake Macquarie, north-west of Sydney, between 1824 and 1859. He was one of the first ethnographers to observe the boomerang in use. Here is his description of the fighting boomerang in use in south-eastern Australia:

*When thrown for the purpose of destruction, whether at man or beast, it is sent forward so as to strike one of its points upon the ground at some distance from the thrower, and the object intended to be hit. The boomerang rebounds, apparently with accelerated velocity, and strikes with astonishing force the victim, inflicting a most serious wound with the sharp edge of the weapon at the flat points. A bomb-shell thrown amongst a company of soldiers cannot create a*

Equipped for battle in the 1890s, a Baadi man of Sunday Island in the Kimberley stands ready, with spears and boomerangs, including one tucked into his hair-string belt. Two engraved pearl-shells also hang from his belt. (C. Ashley, AASAM)

BOTTOM:

A fighting boomerang from Denial Bay on South Australia's west coast, probably obtained from Wirangu people. Note the long panel of deeply fluted carvings. The type has affinities with the long fighting boomerangs of the Gawler Ranges, to the northeast. It was purchased from the prominent Lutheran, Rev. Theodor Nickel, in 1906. 1190 mm. A31939

*greater consternation than the flight of a boomerang towards a group . . . They instantly scatter, and assemble together again the moment the dreaded instrument is seen to have finished its eccentric course. It is thrown in every possible way to damage the enemy; sometimes directly at them, striking the ground first, as described; sometimes it is thrown so as to skim horizontally along close to the ground, or high in the air to take its chance at a venture, but in all instances the boomerang is held with the points towards the object when hurled from the thrower, and happy are they considered who escape from its destructive range. It rips up the individual when it strikes, as though done with a knife, as I witnessed once in my own mare which was accidentally most seriously wounded by the boomerang.* (Gunson (ed.) Vol.1: 69)

The Birdsville Track store-keeper and ethnographer, George Aiston, described the long sword-boomerangs of the region in these terms:

*The koondi [cylindrical boomerang] got longer and flatter until it was no good for throwing, so was developed into a big curved weapon that is used like a two-handed sword. This was anything up to six feet in length and from three to four inches broad. They ranged, in cross*

TOP:

A sharp-angled fighting boomerang from the Broome region, decorated with incised fluting and red-ochred. It was collected during the 1890s by the pearling captain, H.J. Hilliard. His pearling and land-based prospecting trips took him north and south along the Western Australian coast during the 1880s and 1890s. 550 mm. A5360

This long boomerang, with its fine fluted surface, would have been used in hand-to-hand fighting. It is a relic of frontier conflict between Aboriginal people of the northern Flinders Ranges and Europeans. Europeans had moved into the Ranges in large numbers by the 1860s in search of mineral and pastoral wealth. Many Walypi (now known as Adnyamathanha) people continued to live traditionally, relying occasionally upon European sheep to supplement their diet. Punitive raids followed Aboriginal sheep-killing – this boomerang was collected in 1880 during one such raid, on Myrtle Springs station. Donated to the South Australian Museum in 1961 by L.C. Stuart. 1240 mm. A53477

BOTTOM (THIS PAGE):

A broad, open, and sharp-ended style of fighting boomerang typical of the Kimberley region. 620 mm. A16998

section, from perfectly round to a flattened oval. In use they were only for fighting, as their size made them awkward for hunting. They were carried in the belt at the back of the body with the end sticking up over the head of their owner. In a fight, after all of the man's throwing weapons had been discharged, he would grasp the murrawirrie with both hands over his head and, holding it with hands about a foot apart at one end, with the curve downwards, he would use it as a sword, trying to use about only a foot of the end. The result would be that the motion of hitting with it was a drawing stroke when aimed at the chest. The wound usually penetrates into the pleural cavity, if it does not go right through the body. An old fellow, Mundowdna Jack, or Murrapitcheroo,

told me how he fought two men armed with boomerangs and koondi. He used only a murrawirrie. The end of the fight was that he was not touched, one of the others had his skull split, and the other was wounded through the chest wall. Both died at once . . . The murrawirrie was the favourite weapon of the big man, as it needed a lot of strength to wield it properly. The women sometimes used it, possibly because it was frequently left at home as being too bulky to carry. [Horne and Aiston 1924: 72-73]

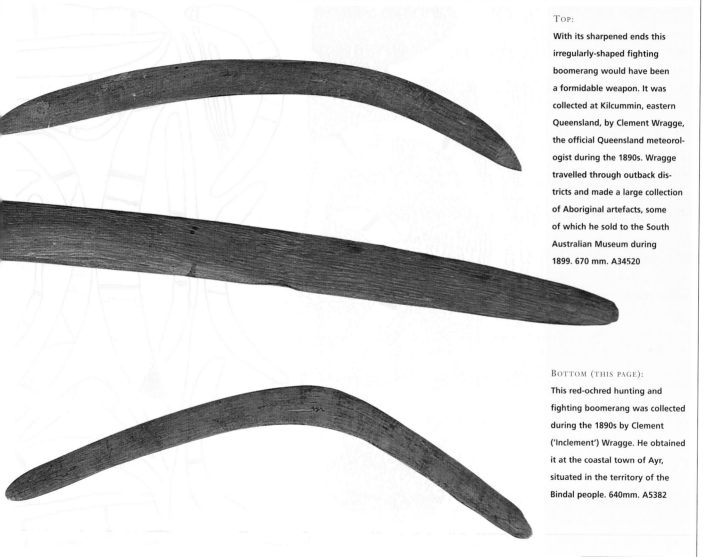

With its sharpened ends this irregularly-shaped fighting boomerang would have been a formidable weapon. It was collected at Kilcummin, eastern Queensland, by Clement Wragge, the official Queensland meteorologist during the 1890s. Wragge travelled through outback districts and made a large collection of Aboriginal artefacts, some of which he sold to the South Australian Museum during 1899. 670 mm. A34520

BOTTOM (THIS PAGE):

This red-ochred hunting and fighting boomerang was collected during the 1890s by Clement ('Inclement') Wragge. He obtained it at the coastal town of Ayr, situated in the territory of the Bindal people. 640mm. A5382

TOP:

Boomerangs of this size, just over a metre in length, were thrown in combat. Larger boomerangs were used as clubs throughout the Lake Eyre region. This boomerang was donated in 1891 by the pastoralist and ethnographic collector, J. Bagot. He obtained it from Aboriginal people at Algebuckina near Oodnadatta, South Australia. 1020 mm. A5449

MIDDLE:

This barely-curved boomerang was used as a fighting weapon by Luritja men in the western MacDonnell Ranges in Central Australia. It was collected during 1929 by H. Heinrich, the schoolteacher at Hermannsburg Lutheran Mission. Heinrich recorded its name as *erama*. Note the finely incised geometric carving over the red-ochred surface, an indication that this boomerang may also have had ritual significance. 1080 mm. A31878

A large fighting boomerang, used in hand-to-hand combat in duels between Aboriginal men of the Diyari, Ngameni, Yawarrawarrka and related groups of the Cooper Creek region in north-eastern South Australia. Senior men kept these long boomerangs close by in their camps. Collected during the early 1900s by Lutheran missionary J.G. Reuther, who subsequently sold a large collection to the South Australian Museum. 1790 mm. A5496

# Hunting Game

A Warlpiri man about to throw
a hunting boomerang at Mt
Denison near Yuendumu in 1931.
The photograph is a reminder
that boomerangs are rarely
thrown from a stationary position. A short run-up of ten metres
or so gives impetus and direction
to the flight. (H.J. Wilkinson, AASAM)

The Aboriginal hunter's ability to direct the flight of the boomerang made it a potent hunting weapon. Much of the skill consisted in stalking game such as emu, kangaroo or other smaller marsupials, and narrowing the distance so that weapons such as boomerangs and spears would be effective. In many cases the boomerang might only stun the animal, allowing the hunter time to kill it by other means. Hunters threw boomerangs directly at their prey, or ricocheted them off the ground, end over end.

Railway worker and naturalist A.G. Bolam gave this account of the hunting boomerang used on the Nullarbor Plain during the 1920s:

*The non-returning boomerang is used in hunting and in fights. An object on the ground – say, a sitting rabbit – is the target, and the boomerang is thrown at it. When it hits the ground, it rises slightly, but the gyratory motion and the shape of the weapon brings it to earth again, and that continues until the force is spent. Anything in the line of flight gets hit, and hurt. I have seen one of these boomerangs thrown a distance of 175 yards, without taking into account the ricochets. It is highly dangerous for a careless spectator to get in the line of fire of a boomerang thrower.* (Bolam 1927: 82)

George Aiston, the Birdsville Track storekeeper and ethnographer, gave this graphic description:

*The force with which a kirra travels was illustrated to me once by a [man] with whom I was travelling. He threw one at a wild turkey that was about fifty yards from him; the kirra struck the branch of a tree about twenty-five yards away. This branch was about two inches in diameter. The kirra cut the branch clean off.* (Aiston 1924: 78)

An Aboriginal man of Stuart's Creek, south of Lake Eyre, about to launch a spear with a spearthrower, and holding boomerangs in one hand. This kit of weapons typically equipped Central Australian Aboriginal men for a day's hunting. (AASAM)

ABOVE:

Queensland Aboriginal man, posed ready to throw a hunting boomerang, ca.1880s (AASAM)

TOP:

This hunting boomerang was collected from the Forrest River in northern Western Australia, close to the northern extent of boomerang distribution. It is a blend of types, marrying the asymmetrical form found throughout the coastal regions to the south with the fluted carvings and ochred surface of Central Australian hunting boomerangs. There are also traces of a painted design on the left wing, with faint bands of yellow ochre and black manganese. The collector was the explorer Charles Price Conigrave, leader of the Kimberley Exploring Expedition of 1911-1912. 780 mm. A622

MIDDLE:

This hunting boomerang may have been made and used by a left-hander. The longer and straighter arm is likely to have been the one gripped by the thrower, a Nyangumarta man. Norman Tindale collected this boomerang in 1953 at Djingano, east of Mandora, south of Broome, Western Australia. The slight asymmetry of the wings conforms with coastal styles, while the ochred and fluted surface suggests the influence of the desert country to the east. This influence is reinforced by its Nyangumarta name, *karli*, a term for boomerang used throughout much of Australia's Western Desert. 630 mm. A45206

BOTTOM:

The size and asymmetrical shape of this Flinders Ranges hunting boomerang is similar to those of Central Australia. There are significant differences though: the sharpened attacking end, the unochred and plain surface, and the roughened handgrip. This example was collected by Tom Hunter in the northern Flinders Ranges during the 1880s. By this time, Aboriginal people in the Ranges were finding it increasingly difficult to maintain their traditional hunting and gathering existence. 520 mm. A51170

TOP:

An important example of a hunting boomerang from the Narungga people of Yorke Peninsula, collected in about 1895. By this time the Narungga had mostly contracted to the Point Pearce mission station at the north of the peninsula. Most of their traditional hunting territory had been alienated by European settlement, and the native animals which they had hunted had largely disappeared. This boomerang, made of sheoak timber, is a link between the larger, heavier boomerangs used to the north and west of Yorke Peninsula, and the flatter and broader types used to the south-east. It was collected by Hanley, a telegraph station operator. 540 mm. A34200

MIDDLE:

A typical example of a Central Australian hunting boomerang. The fresh-looking coat of red ochre and the panel of yellow ochre at one end suggests that the boomerang was also used in ceremony. Traces of a Dreaming design in black charcoal are also evident on this panel. Sold to the South Australian Museum in 1904 by the one-legged telegraph operator, James Field, this boomerang was probably obtained at Tennant Creek from a Warlpiri or Warumungu man. 680mm. A5409

BOTTOM:

This undecorated boomerang with its sharpened ends would have been a lethal hunting and fighting weapon. A roughened hand-grip can be seen at the base of the longest arm. Collected in eastern Queensland during one of his tours of duty during the 1890s by government meteorologist Clement Wragge. 620 mm. A34664

# Hunting Birds

Aboriginal people used returning and non-returning boomerangs to hunt birds. In south-eastern Australia in particular, returning boomerangs were used to hunt water-birds. A returning boomerang was thrown above a flock of ducks to simulate a hawk, hovering and ready to snatch its prey. The ducks would fly low to avoid this threat, coming within range of hunters' clubs or tangling themselves in nets stretched across waterways.

Aboriginal hunters also threw non-returning boomerangs into dense flocks of birds such as parrots, often killing more than one. The hooked boomerangs of northern Central Australia were particularly effective in this way.

**This artist's impression shows a group of hunters frightening ducks along a waterway towards nets they had set.** (G. Aldrdidge, AASAM)

The Yandruwandha man, Benny Kerwin, gave a unique account of hunting ducks with nets and boomerangs on the Cooper Creek at Innamincka. Interviewed by the linguist Gavan Breen in 1972, Kerwin described a practice which he had seen in his youth, in about 1900. It is the only account which suggests that returning boomerangs were regularly used in eastern Central Australia, and the only account to mention the strategy of boring a hole in one end of a boomerang so that it 'whistled' like a hawk. Other accounts, from south-eastern Australia, describe how the hunters themselves gave a 'whistle' or 'cry' to simulate the noise of the hawk.

Benny Kerwin: *If they want to catch birds (ie ducks) they make a net of a different mesh and tie it on to a tree on each bank of the river. The net is big enough so that it goes right from a tree nearby to a big coolibah standing on the other side, and they tie it on over there.*

*Then they take a boomerang, and they put a hole in the end of it [so that it will whistle when it is thrown]. Then a lot of men go and chase the birds down.*

*Well, when the birds fly down to the net, the men waiting there on both sides of the river throw their boomerangs. The birds dive down.*

Gavan Breen: *What for?*

Benny Kerwin: *Because they think it is a chicken hawk, and they go into the net. Then two men throw the net down and pull it in. They get many birds.*

*That's how the Aboriginals used to catch birds to eat, with a special net they had woven.*

(Translated extract, Hercus & Sutton 1986:33)

The explorer Captain George Grey wrote this eyewitness account of the use of returning boomerangs by people of south-western Western Australia, probably based on his own experiences at King George Sound during 1839:

*Perhaps as fine a sight as can be seen in the whole circle of native sports is the killing [of] cockatoos with the kiley, or boomerang. A [hunter] perceived a large flight of cockatoos in a forest which encircles a lagoon; the expanse of water affords an open clear space above it, unencumbered with trees, but which raise their gigantic forms all around . . . and in their leafy*

**Returning boomerangs made from sheoak, arranged to show curvature and motion in flight. Boomerangs like these from south-eastern Australia were used for hunting waterbirds. (AASAM)**

A posed photograph of an unidentified Aboriginal man, demonstrating bird-hunting with a boomerang. Photographed in Charles Kerry's studio, Sydney, 1880s. (AASAM)

RIGHT:
Thrown into a flock of parrots or ducks rising from an inland waterhole, hooked boomerangs like this were used to devastating effect. It was collected by the Barrow Creek telegraph station master, Hanley, during the early 1890s. 760 mm. A34203

summits sit a countless number of cockatoos, screaming and flying from tree to tree, as they make their arrangements for a night's sound sleep. The [hunter] throws aside his cloak, so that he may not even have this slight covering to impede his motions, draws his kiley from his belt and, with a noiseless, elastic step, approaches the lagoon, creeping from tree to tree, from bush to bush, and disturbing the birds as little as possible; their sentinels, however, take the alarm, the cockatoos farthest from the water fly to the trees near its edge, and thus they keep concentrating their forces . . . they are aware that danger is at hand but are ignorant of its nature. At length, the pursuer almost reaches the edge of the water, and the scared cockatoos, with wild cries, spring into the air; at the same instant the [hunter] raises his right hand high over his shoulder, and, bounding forward with his utmost speed for a few paces, to give impetus to his blow, the kiley quits his hand as if it would strike the water, but when it has almost touched the unruffled surface of the lake, it spins upwards, with inconceivable velocity, and with the strangest contortions. In vain the terrified cockatoos strive to avoid it; it sweeps wildly and uncertainly through the air, and so eccentric are its motions, that it requires but a slight stretch of imagination to fancy it endowed with life, and with fell swoops is in rapid pursuit of the devoted birds – some of whom are almost certain to be brought screaming to the earth.

But the wily [hunter] has not yet done with them. He avails himself of the extraordinary attachment which these birds have for one another, and, fastening a wounded one to a tree, so that its cries may induce its companions to return, he watches his opportunity by throwing his kiley or spear to add another bird or two to the booty he has already obtained. (Grey 1841: 281-282)

**TOP:**

An unusually shaped boomerang, obtained from Aboriginal people of northern Western Australia during 1916 by the doctor, explorer and anthropologist, Herbert Basedow. It was described by him as a returning boomerang. If that is so, it was probably used for hunting birds. Its banded decoration of red and white ochre over a finely-fluted surface indicates that it may also have been used in a ceremonial context. 550 mm. A21530

**BOTTOM:**

Made of a light wood, possibly mangrove, this boomerang would not have been heavy enough to use in hunting large animals. Its main function may have been in hunting birds. Collected during the 1890s by Queensland meteorologist Clement Wragge from the coastal district near Nambour, north of Brisbane. 530 mm. A39576

**SECOND FROM TOP:**

A returning boomerang made of sheoak wood, used by Aboriginal people of south-eastern South Australia. Returning boomerangs of this type were used for hunting waterbirds – thrown out at a critical moment over a flock of ducks the boomerang's hovering flight would frighten the birds down, within range of hunters with clubs, spears or nets. Otherwise, the boomerang is heavy enough to have killed one or more birds if thrown directly into a flock. If it missed the birds, it would return to the thrower. Obtained from Dr O.H. Selling in 1949, but probably dating from at least the 1880s. 520 mm. A9612

**THIRD FROM TOP:**

Typical sheoak returning boomerang from south-eastern South Australia or Victoria, probably used for waterbird hunting. Purchased at Johnson's Auction Mart, ca.1905. 460 mm. A5386

# Fishing with a Boomerang

Fish-killing boomerangs are known from only two localities in Australia – the Broome region of north-western Australia, and Port Lincoln on South Australia's west coast. Both regions are noted for high daily tidal variations, which leave fish stranded in tidal pools. Aboriginal hunters stood above these pools and used heavy, broad boomerangs to slice through the water and kill fish. The practice extended to rivers, and to the long surf beaches of the Kimberley coast. Following the arrival of Europeans, Aboriginal people of the Broome region experimented with metal boomerangs for the same purpose.

The South Australian Museum anthropologist Norman Tindale described the fish-killing boomerang in these terms:

*A further type of boomerang is the specialised fish killer, which has not been noticed often by ethnographers. Its distinguishing characteristic is that it is symetrically biconvex in section and is usually heavy. It is cast into tidal waters to kill larger types of fish and other marine animals, then retrieved when the tide ebbs.*

(Tindale 1974: 108)

Anthropologist Stanley Porteus visited Beagle Bay Mission in the Kimberley during the late 1920s. His account of fishing boomerangs indicates that they were used in inland creeks as well as in the ocean, although by the 1920s modified iron examples were being used:

*. . . fish in the creek are speared or killed with a boomerang cut out of old sheet iron. These are called 'tanks' and are hurled with great force and accuracy into the water when a large fish is descried near the surface.* (Porteus 1931: 10)

Visiting German ethnographer E. Clement observed the Kimberley fishing boomerang in use during the 1890s. Examples collected by him are in German museums. He wrote:

*In shallow water, the fish are killed by throwing the* kaili *at them, when they are five or six inches below the surface.*
(Clement 1903: 3)

Aboriginal people of the Broome region continued to fish with boomerangs after the Europeans brought metal to the area. Metal boomerangs were recorded as early as the 1890s and were used until the 1960s. Very few were collected by museums – this example, cut from sheet metal by a Nyangumarta man, was obtained in 1953 by Norman Tindale at Mandora Station, close to the 80 Mile Beach. Tindale recorded its name as *korolinj*. 450 mm. A45163

LEFT:
This photograph, taken during 1996, shows the Baadi man, Henry Hunter, demonstrating the use of a Kimberley fishing boomerang. (W. Barker)

# Boomerangs and Fire

The boomerang has been called the 'Swiss Army Knife' of Aboriginal Australia, but you can't make fire with a Swiss Army Knife! For many Aboriginal groups, particularly through Central Australia and north Western Australia, the hunting boomerang was routinely employed as a fire-making tool. Rubbed to and fro at speed across a softwood surface, such as a beantree shield, the sharp edge of a boomerang generates enough heat to cause a spark, lighting tinder such as dry bark or grass. Many Central Australian boomerangs in museum collections bear the tell-tale singe marks of fire-making along their outer edges.

Boomerangs were also used for tending fires. They were ideal implements for raking out coals to prepare a cooking surface, and for digging fire-pits for cooking.

A Wangkangurru man making fire by rubbing the edge of a boomerang rapidly backwards and forwards across a softwood shield. The friction would eventually produce a spark, spreading to the dry grass used as tinder. Photographed at Mungeranie, east of Lake Eyre, in about 1920.

(G. Aiston, AASAM)

**TOP:**

An unochred hunting and fighting boomerang, collected in 1897 at the coastal town of Geraldton, Western Australia, by C.M.G. Elliot. The top left and bottom right edges are charred, indicating use for making fire by friction against a softwood surface, such as a shield. 530 mm. A5374

**MIDDLE:**

A fine example of a valued and well-used Central Australian boomerang, used both as a fire-making implement and as a poker. Aboriginal men used boomerangs of this type to make fire, by rubbing the edge of the boomerang at speed across a groove in the surface of a softwood shield. The friction eventually caused a spark, setting tinder alight. Slight charring on the top surface of the boomerang indicates that it was used for this function; the charred end is evidence of the boomerang's use for tending fires. The owner valued this boomerang enough to repair a split with binding made from the tendons of a kangaroo. The boomerang was obtained in 1891 from Luritja or Arrernte people by R. F. Thornton, manager of Tempe Downs station, west of Alice Springs. 710 mm. A5408

**BOTTOM:**

This boomerang, collected in the Alice Springs district by H. Sheard during 1939, has given long service as a fire-tending tool. The charring along the top and bottom edges also indicates its use as a fire-making 'saw', used in conjunction with a softwood shield and dry grass as tinder. A hole in the boomerang has been plugged with spinifex resin. Sheard recorded its Arrernte name as *ulbarinja*. 650 mm. A28306

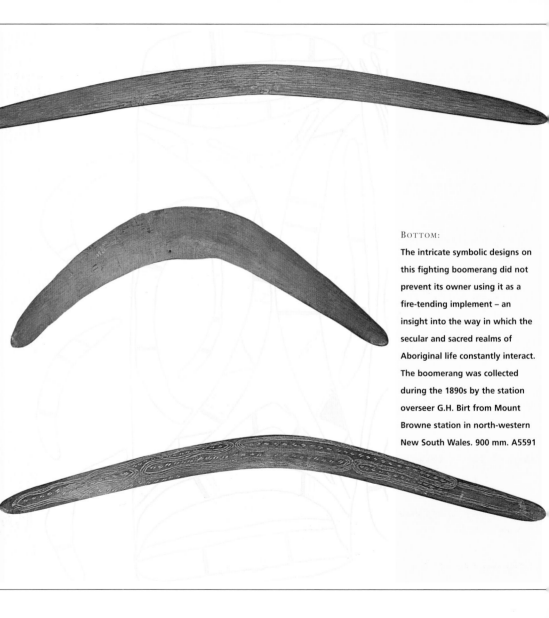

TOP:

The blackened ends of this long fighting boomerang indicate its use as a fire poker. The boomerang was obtained during the 1870s by Barossa Valley naturalist Marianne Kreusler from Aboriginal people passing through Gawler, possibly on their way to Adelaide. This ochred and fluted example suggests an influence from the north of South Australia, perhaps the Lake Torrens and Lake Eyre districts. 930 mm. A50859

MIDDLE:

In contrast to the multi-purpose Central Australian boomerangs, those from south-eastern Australia were more restricted in their function. With its charred tip, this sheoak boomerang from Lake Alexandrina in South Australia provides an exception. It was probably used for tending fires as well as for hunting, prior to its collection by the missionary George Taplin, perhaps as early as the 1860s. 560 mm. A5282

BOTTOM:

The intricate symbolic designs on this fighting boomerang did not prevent its owner using it as a fire-tending implement – an insight into the way in which the secular and sacred realms of Aboriginal life constantly interact. The boomerang was collected during the 1890s by the station overseer G.H. Birt from Mount Browne station in north-western New South Wales. 900 mm. A5591

TOP:

Charring at both ends reveals this boomerang's use as an all-purpose tool around the campfire. It was originally collected by Lutheran missionary Oskar Liebler at Hermannsburg, Northern Territory, in 1910 and was subsequently acquired by the South Australian Museum through Adelaide merchant F.G. Scarfe. 600 mm. A555

MIDDLE:

This hooked boomerang was collected in 1891 by Mrs T. Evans of Pine Creek, north of Katherine in the Northern Territory. It was probably traded from further south. Once decorated for ceremony, the black outline of the Dreaming design has been largely obliterated. The charred handle indicates its use as a fire-tending implement. 730 mm. A5457

BOTTOM:

A fine example of an all-purpose Central Australian boomerang made of mulga (Acacia aneura). While its primary use may have been for hunting, this type of boomerang filled a wide range of functions. Its use as a fire tool is evident, and the broad end has been sharpened, making an effective knife for butchering meat. Norman Tindale bartered for this in 1931 with Kakuda, a Warlpiri man, at Yulumu, west of Lander Creek in Central Australia. The fluted carving is lightly coloured with red ochre. Tindale noted that Warlpiri boomerangs are characterised by a slight widening of the shorter arm. 630 mm. A15777

# Performance and Music

When they entered the territory of Aboriginal groups in Central and Western Australia during the nineteenth century, European explorers were often intimidated by Aboriginal men waving and rattling boomerangs. The explorers were unaware that these displays were often ritual greetings.

Boomerangs are still an integral part of ceremonial dances in Central and Northern Australia. In the Warlpiri Fire Ceremony, for example, a line of men decorated with headdresses and body paint wave boomerangs aloft as they enter the ceremonial ground, lit by fires. Boomerangs figure in illustrations of Aboriginal ceremony from south-eastern Australia, recorded early in the nineteenth century. Rare photographs of Bora ceremonies from eastern Australia, dating to the 1890s, show ceremonial grounds marked with lines of boomerangs stuck into the ground.

Aboriginal performers still use boomerangs as musical percussion instruments in Central and Northern Australia. A pair of hunting boomerangs is clapped or rattled together to maintain or vary the rhythm of ceremonial song. Boomerangs are used in this way even in parts of north and north-western Australia where they are not known as hunting weapons. In Central Australia performers also use boomerangs as percussion instruments by slapping them on the ground, producing a deep resonant note.

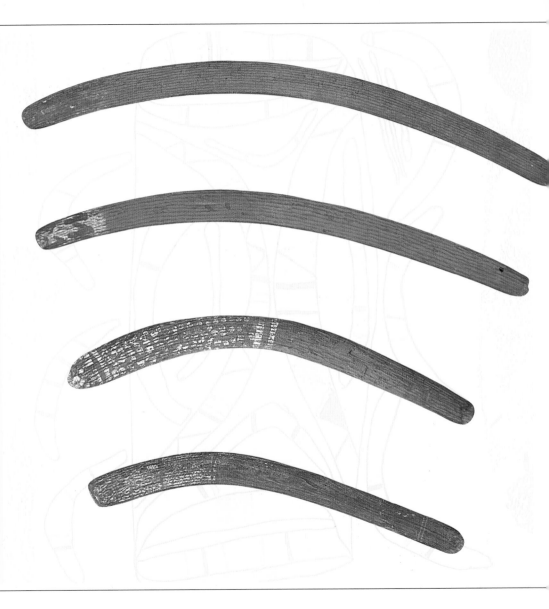

TOP:

The smudged designs on this pair of boomerangs represent the tracks of Dreaming Kangaroos. It is likely that these two boomerangs, collected from Aboriginal people more than a century ago at the Daly Waters telegraph station, were once a pair. They were probably used as clapsticks or time-beating instruments in a Kangaroo Ceremony. These Dreamings and associated ceremonies are still known and practised in the region today. The collector was probably Frederick Goss, the Daly Waters telegraph stationmaster. 770 mm; 730 mm. A34611; A34632

BOTTOM:

This pair of boomerangs originated in northern Central Australia and was traded north to the Maung people of Goulburn Island. Here they were painted with designs evoking Dreamings of the region and were used as clapsticks in ceremonies. The boomerangs were collected during the 1920s by missionary Margaret Matthews. 560mm; 570 mm. A41580; A41582

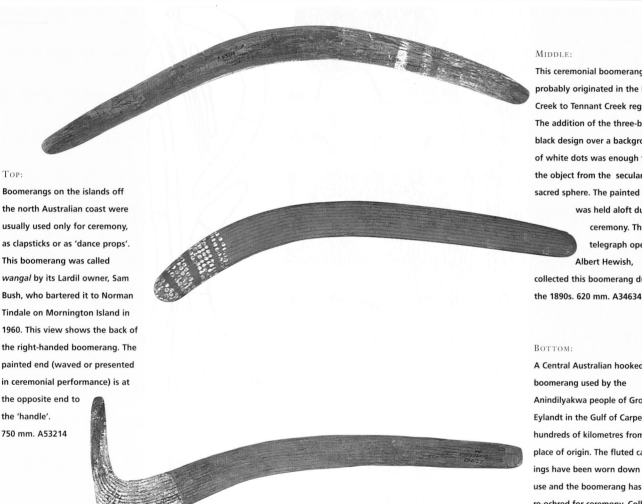

**MIDDLE:**

This ceremonial boomerang probably originated in the Barrow Creek to Tennant Creek region. The addition of the three-barred black design over a background of white dots was enough to shift the object from the secular to the sacred sphere. The painted end was held aloft during ceremony. The telegraph operator, Albert Hewish, collected this boomerang during the 1890s. 620 mm. A34634

**TOP:**

Boomerangs on the islands off the north Australian coast were usually used only for ceremony, as clapsticks or as 'dance props'. This boomerang was called *wangal* by its Lardil owner, Sam Bush, who bartered it to Norman Tindale on Mornington Island in 1960. This view shows the back of the right-handed boomerang. The painted end (waved or presented in ceremonial performance) is at the opposite end to the 'handle'. 750 mm. A53214

**BOTTOM:**

A Central Australian hooked boomerang used by the Anindilyakwa people of Groote Eylandt in the Gulf of Carpentaria, hundreds of kilometres from its place of origin. The fluted carvings have been worn down with use and the boomerang has been re-ochred for ceremony. Collected by Dr D.R. Brown in 1930. 680 mm. A20073

Most languages of Central Australia have a particular term for the sound of boomerangs being rattled together. In the Alyawarr language, for example, the term is *alterrp kwelheyel*. In the Pintupi/Luritja language, the term for tapping boomerangs rhythmically together at ceremonies is *timpilpungu*. This noise is also made as a signal to call people together for a ceremony.

BELOW:

Three dancers performing a ceremonial hunt using boomerangs, photographed in New South Wales during the 1880s. (C. Kerry, AASAM)

OPPOSITE PAGE:

Ancient cultural themes such as the origin and role of the boomerang are being explored afresh by a new generation of Aboriginal artists and performers. The Ngarrindjeri–Narungga Dreaming dance troupe was founded in 1992 by Carroll Karpany and draws its inspiration from the shared Aboriginal heritage of the Lower Murray River and Yorke Peninsula. The company performs regularly at Uluru (Ayers Rock) and has toured nationally and internationally. This photograph shows the troupe performing the Boomerang Dance (The Creation of the Boomerang and the Celebration of the Boomerang), against the backdrop of the Murray River. (C. Karpany)

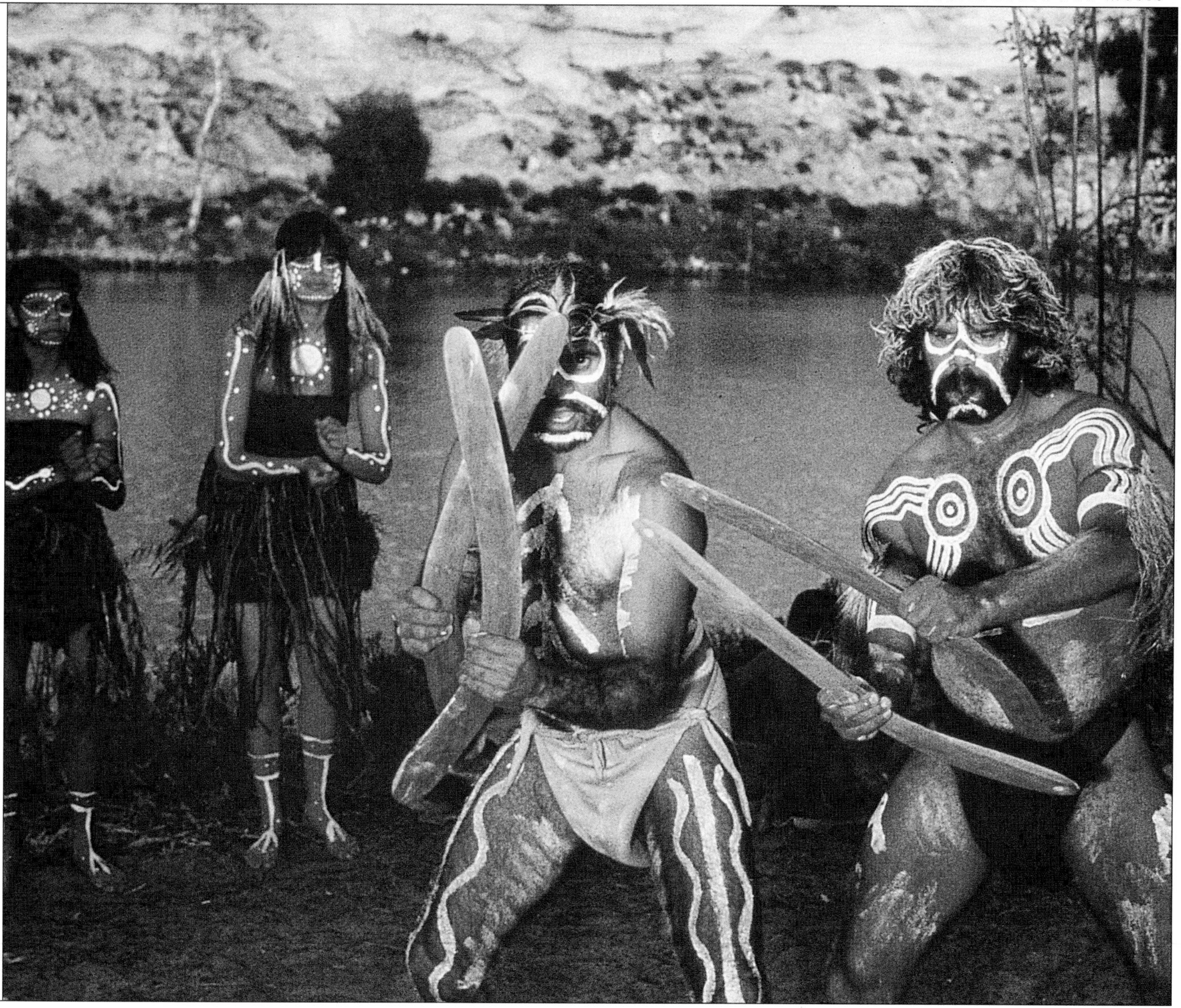

TOP:

This rare form of hooked boomerang presents a problem for ethnographers – there is no direct evidence of it having been used for fighting or hunting and it has been found in only two, widely separated regions – Cooper Creek in north-eastern South Australia, and Roper River in the Northern Territory. Painted forms of this boomerang were known to have had a ceremonial function in the Cooper Creek region. Edward Stirling, director of the South Australian Museum, collected this decorated boomerang during his 1899 expedition to the Warburton River. 790 mm.
A5528

MIDDLE:

A 1940s Flinders Ranges boomerang carved by Davey Ryan, decorated with a ceremonial scene showing women singing and clapping boomerangs to accompany male dancers. A61408

BOTTOM:

This ceremonial boomerang, painted with ochres and manganese, was collected in 1891 by pastoralist John Bagot at Algebuckina, on the Lake Eyre Basin. It is similar in form to those of the Cooper Creek region to the east. 840 mm.  A5535

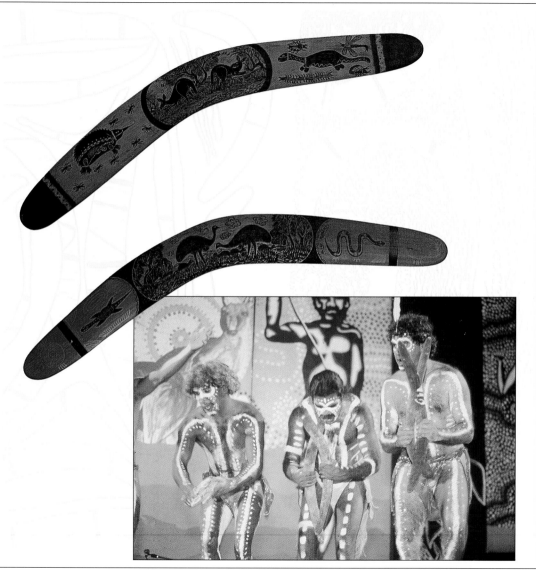

The South Australian Aboriginal artist, Bluey Roberts, has been associated with the Ngarrindjeri-Narungga dance troupe since its inception, and his traditional chant accompanies the performance of the Boomerang Dance. In carving the two boomerangs depicted here, Bluey drew on his mother's Ngarrindjeri ancestry to depict the animals and spirit ancestors. He has singed the designs onto the wooden surfaces, a technique used by his father's people, from the west coast of South Australia. Bluey is an accomplished boomerang thrower and has competed successfully in national competitions. He has exhibited his work in Japan, and has even given boomerang workshops there. 740mm, 640 mm (B. Roberts)

The Ngarrindjeri–Narungga dance troupe performing their Boomerang Dance at Tandanya, the National Aboriginal Cultural Institute in Adelaide (C. Karpany)

# Trade in Boomerangs

Two of the main boomerang types were traded extensively across large regions of Australia.

The heavy ornate boomerangs of the Darling/Cooper river systems were traded east along the river into the central regions of Queensland and New South Wales, and west as far as the MacDonnell Ranges.

The hooked boomerangs of north-central Australia (Tennant Creek vicinity) were traded south as far as the MacDonnell Ranges, west as far as the Kimberley, north to the Gulf of Carpentaria and east into Queensland. These hooked boomerangs were often traded in pairs. In Arnhem Land and the Kimberley they were regarded as sacred objects.

Trade in boomerangs was motivated partly by demand for particular types, but boomerangs were also traded in the course of social contacts or in exchange for commodities such as Flinders Ranges red ochre or the pituri narcotic of western Queensland.

Returning boomerangs were apparently not traded, – an irony, given that it is returning boomerangs that are made for mass sale today.

The Queensland ethnographer, Walter Roth, was one of several commentators to record the fact that boomerangs were often made and traded in pairs:

*It is interesting to note that both in camp or on the walk-about, though an Aboriginal may carry one spear, one shield, etc, he almost invariably has two boomerangs. If they have been made by the same person they are probably similarly marked: if he barters them he will generally 'swap' them only as a pair, though beyond the fact of two being required as an accompaniment for beating time at the singsongs and the corrobborees, it is difficult to understand why this should so often be the case.* (Roth 1897: 143)

Anthropologist Mervyn Meggitt observed that boomerangs were still being used as exchange items during marriage negotiations among the Warlpiri of the Tanami Desert, during the 1950s. He wrote:

*The public ceremony of betrothal occurs when the girl is between six and eighteen months old. The father and maternal kinsmen of the young man decide that his djuraldja line (his future wife's matriline) must now meet its obligation, and one of the men warns the girl's father or mother's brother of this. Close cognates of the suitor help him to accumulate the bride-price. In the past this included such things as cooked meat (especially kangaroo and emu), pieces of red-ochre, skeins of hair-string, boomerangs, hunting and fighting spears, spearthrowers and softwood shields – articles readily available to all men in the society. Nowadays, clothes, cloth, blankets and money are also acceptable.*

This hooked boomerang, originating in the Warlpiri or Warumungu territories of northern Central Australia, was traded south-east to the Arrernte of the MacDonnell Ranges. The Arrernte did not make hooked boomerangs and they were rarely seen in the region when Europeans first arrived there. As the frequency of European travel throughout Central Australia increased, so did the opportunities for trade and social contact between Aboriginal groups which had previously never mingled. The boomerang was collected in 1929 by Norman Tindale, through the Hermannsburg mission schoolteacher, H.A. Heinrich. 620 mm. A17432

Meggitt gave the following example:

*Larry djungarai gave one pound, six blankets, six spears and eight boomerangs to the father of his first wife and one pound to her mother's mother.* (Meggit 1962: 266-267)

Boomerangs were apparently not used in the Adelaide area at the time of European arrival. Writing in 1845, George French Angas noted that boomerangs were introduced to the region by New South Wales Aboriginal people who may have accompanied droving parties to Adelaide along the Murray River. He wrote:

*They were occasionally found in the Encampments; supposed to have been procured from the New South Wales Natives, and passed from one tribe to another in the way of barter, or as presents.* (Angas 1847: plate 6, no.5)

This account of trading in the Broome region of north-western Australia was recorded by the anthropologist Daisy Bates, and applies to the early 1900s:

*Jajjala man and his friends will elect to make a certain number of weapons for barter with tribes north, south, east or west. Karrboorna kanna ballee, ngai inna kanna ballee (shield [will] make, I will make), will be the remark of a young man; joo na wan ballee lanjee (you make boomerang), he tells another. Maaboo kanna ballee, panderr jinna maaboo (good make it, markings make good), and so they proceed to make a bundle of their own manufacture. When all are made and have the ancestral or totem markings on them, the messenger is chosen from the group sending the bundle for barter. He is charged with a message which may be as follows 'I send you a little bundle, I haven't got much, I will get more by and by'. All the articles will be marked with either the totem mark of the maker or with ancestral designs which any of the young men can make on shield or boomerang. The articles that might be sent from Jajjala would include shields, ceremonial flat pointed sticks, clubs, three kinds of boomerang, hairstring, carved pearlshell, red ochre, dark yellow, yellow and white earths, and stone belonging to Jajjala ground only. These would probably be sent to 'brothers', 'uncles', or 'fathers' living north, who would examine the weapons, and seeing the markings would say 'Jajjala man's making, painting, marking, etc.' If the weapons were also painted with red and white they would be alluded to as 'painted with red and white'.*

*The people to the north would send back in exchange pipeshell necklaces, necklaces made of human hair and kangaroo teeth attached with gum, necklaces made of dogs' tails and flying fox fur, arranged button fashion, large pearlshells, grooved and painted, local spears, and some Northern red ochre and white pipeclay.*

*. . . the articles may be taken east, when the Jajjala people will receive in return chisels or chipped spearheads, also another kind of chipped flint spearheads, two kinds of boomerang, shields made from the* joonboo *tree [etc.]* (Bates 1985: 285)

Through the influence of trade and the social contacts accompanying it, no Aboriginal community in mainland Australia was isolated from its neighbours and their influences. The pair of boomerangs pictured on this page reflects that fact. They were collected in 1938 at Lake Nash, near the Northern Territory and Queensland border. The Lake Nash region received boomerangs in trade from Central Australia to the west and from the Lake Eyre region to the south. The top boomerang was owned by an Alyawarr man of Lake Nash and is typical of those traded from the west. The bottom example, with its incised decorations, was also owned by an Alyawarr man. It was probably traded to Lake Nash from the Diamantina River region to the south. 660 mm; 830 mm. A27456; A27457

# Boomerangs in Aboriginal Sport

**A boomerang-throwing contest in the late nineteenth century, depicted in a lithograph by S.Tilby.**

Both non-returning and returning boomerangs were used for sport in Aboriginal Australia, the former in contests for the furthest distance thrown. In games involving returning boomerangs, competitors would try to make their boomerang return within a circle drawn on the ground or to strike a peg.

A game in the Boulia region of south-west Queensland involved a line of six or seven men standing in Indian file with their hands on each other's shoulders. Each would take turns to throw a returning boomerang; the others would try to avoid being hit, swaying from side to side. Other boomerang sports involved exhibitions of skill, throwing the boomerang in figures of eight or long loops, with it sometimes even touching the ground before returning.

This account was recorded in south-western Victoria by James Dawson:

OPPOSITE PAGE:
**Expert Harry Williams retrieves a high-flying boomerang before an apprehensive gallery. From the front cover of *Walkabout* magazine, July 1963.**

*Sometimes a fight takes place in the form of a tournament or friendly trial of skill in the use of the boomerang and shield. Ten or twelve warriors, painted with white stripes across the cheeks and nose, and armed with shields and boomerangs, are met by an equal number at a distance of about twenty paces. Each individual has a right to throw his boomerang at anyone on the other*

**This boomerang, apparently conforming to the ordinary non-returning style of Central Australia, has been documented as a returning boomerang. Norman Tindale, described the details of its manufacture and flight during a 1930 expedition among the Anmatyerre people of eastern Central Australia during 1930. 480 mm. A14895**

*side, and steps out of the rank into the intervening space to do so. The opposite party take their turn, and so on alternately, until someone is hit, or all are satisfied. Every warrior has a boy to look after his boomerang, which, on striking a shield, flies up and falls at a considerable distance. As the boomerang is thrown with great force, it requires very great dexterity and quick sight to ward off such an erratic weapon, and affords a fine opportunity for displaying the remarkable activity of the aborigines. This activity is, no doubt, considerably roused by fear of the severe cut which is inflicted by the boomerang. Mourners are not allowed to join in these tournaments, as it would be considered disrespectful to the dead. Women and children are generally kept at a safe distance. The chiefs and aged warriors stand by to see fair play, and to stop the proceedings when they think they have gone far enough.* [Dawson 1881: 77-78]

The following account of organised boomerang-throwing competitions among the Ngarrindjeri groups of the Murray Lakes region in South Australia was published by William Ramsay Smith in 1930. Smith drew upon the knowledge, if not the actual manuscript, of the Aboriginal writer and inventor, David Unaipon, who is portrayed on Australia's fifty dollar note. Unaipon had a particular interest in the returning boomerang's aerodynamic properties and experimented with his own models.

*Boomerang-throwing is another great sport. This is a game in which men of fifty years of age will take part, as well as young men and boys. The Turtle tribe may send a challenge to all the surrounding tribes within a range of three or four hundred miles. On a calm, clear day a smoke-signal is sent up, and a message is sent that the Turtle tribe has made a number of boomerangs that cannot be equalled for quality. All the tribes are challenged to come and test them. They are invited to a certain place, on the shores of Lake Albert, where there are plains free from trees or shrubs. Now, for a busy fortnight, each tribe is engaged in making and testing their boomerangs. Then they come out on the ground, fully equipped, their bodies painted after various fashions, and their boomerangs carved in a variety of designs representing their tribe. A Turtle tribe man is the first to perform with his boomerang. Perhaps it is made to circle round him three times before hovering about his head and descending to the earth within two or three yards of where he stands. A Goanna tribe man will next accept the challenge and enter the ring. He throws his boomerang, and it goes in a straight course from him for about seventy yards, and then gradually works itself round and passes across the line at about forty yards, travelling in a spiral towards the performer. Next time it passes the line it comes within twenty yards; then it comes nearer, until it hovers about the Goanna man, and spins until its energy is exhausted. It touches the earth, and falls inside a circle about two feet from where the thrower stands.* (Smith 1930: 241)

Boomerangs of this type were used for hunting waterfowl, as well as in games and competitions, in south-eastern Australia. This example, from the Mount Gambier district of South Australia, was collected by the local mayor, Francis Davison, probably during the 1870s. 470 mm. A15704

# Toy Boomerangs

As soon as they were old enough to run after them, Aboriginal boys across Australia played with boomerangs. In fact, it is possible that their experiments with toy boomerangs actually led to the invention of the returning boomerang, many centuries ago.

As well as the sheer fun of playing with them, boys used their miniature boomerangs to imitate the hunting exploits of their elders. Adult men often made small boomerangs for their boys to use, providing vital training for later bush life.

Aboriginal boys threw returning boomerangs in games and competitions, particularly in eastern and south-eastern Australia. Early settler accounts tell of adults and children lighting the ends of returning boomerangs and then hurling them through the night sky, making a spectacular path. Children often made their own toy boomerangs, experimenting with pieces of curved bark until they acquired the wood-carving skills needed to make finely-tuned boomerangs. In the Cardwell region, south of Cairns, Aboriginal children played with cross-boomerangs of various shapes and materials, even reeds.

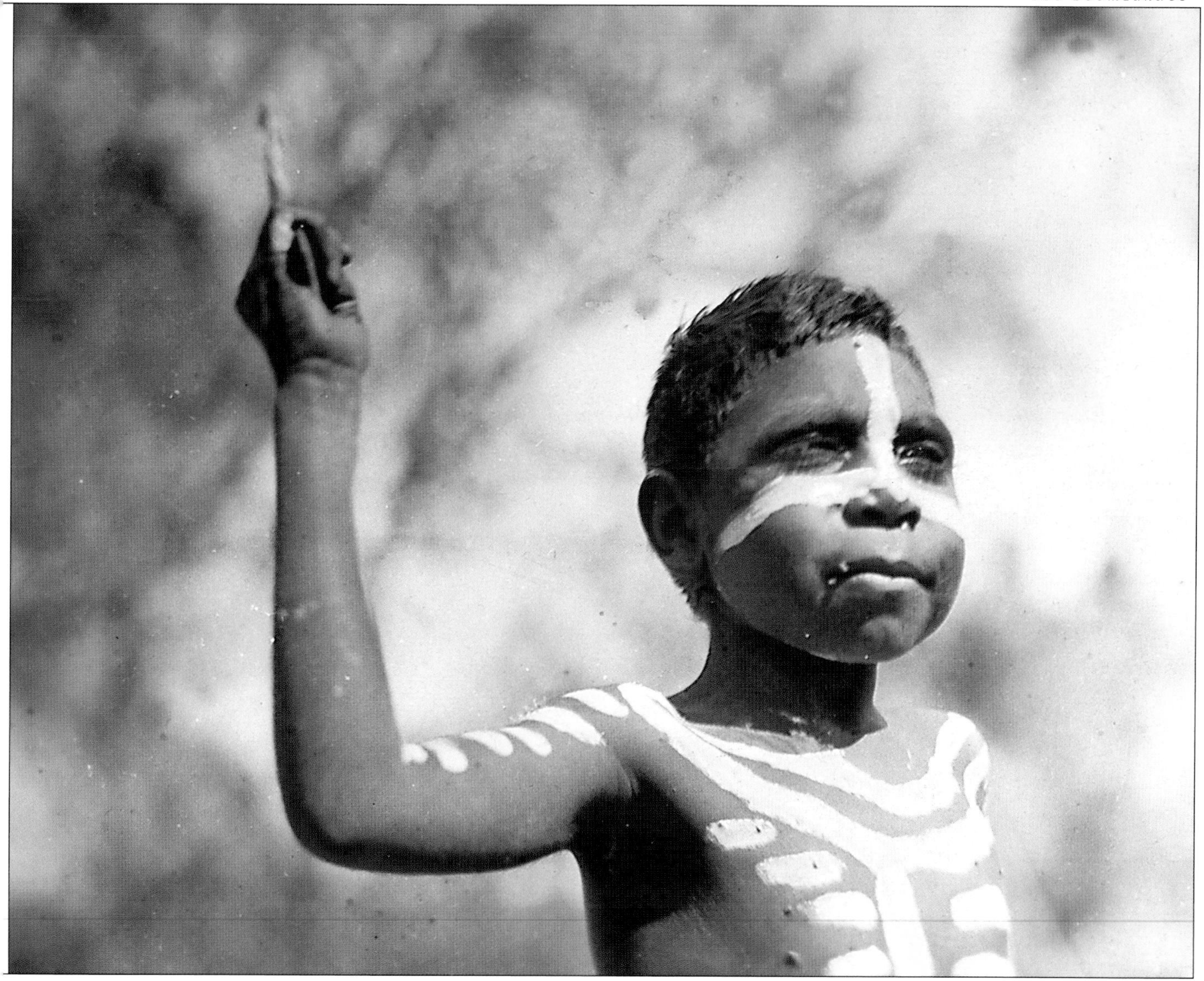

This extract is from a newspaper article written during an anthropological expedition to Mount Liebig, Central Australia, during August 1932:

*In one popular game [the boys] use tiny boomerangs, which trains them for the time when they will have to take their places as warriors with their tribe.*

*The boys divide into two sides and separate about 30 yards in a cleared patch. They then hurl the boomerangs at one another. When a boy is hit he drops out of the game as if he were killed. The side that has most left at the end wins.*

*They try to let the boomerangs come as close as possible without being hit, and skilfully dodge and twist to let the missiles whirl past harmlessly. The game is often kept up for a long time. The boys shout and laugh, and never seem to tire.*

*The boomerangs are made to skip at great speed along the ground, and the boys are very delighted if they can borrow a shield from their men to catch their opponents' shots.*

*The older boys use real boomerangs, and learn to catch them in full flight. They also practise with blunted spears, hurling them at each other.*

(N.B. Tindale. Mt Liebig Journal, AASAM)

**This small boomerang is an enigma. It was collected in 1885 by the author Arthur Vogan on Thursday Island in the Torres Strait, where boomerangs have not otherwise been recorded. From its size and shape this is likely to have been a child's returning boomerang.**
**It may have been brought to Thursday Island by Aboriginal people working in the Torres Strait pearling industry.**
**400 mm. A2862**

FRONT

BACK

TOP:

This unochred boomerang was made by a Ngalea adult as a toy for a young boy at Yalata, South Australia. In traditional times, the time spent by boys playing with boomerangs like this example provided vital preparation for later life. Collected by anthropologist Norman B. Tindale in 1965. 270 mm. A60678

BOTTOM:

This Central Australian boy's boomerang was made by a a Kukatja man. It is painted with traditional designs in European paints. Collected by R.G. Kimber in 1979. 340 mm. A66804

MIDDLE LEFT:

This boy's boomerang probably had the capacity to return. In areas where they were rarely used by adults, such as Central Australia or the Western Desert, returning boomerangs were often made for children as playthings. Few of them have been preserved in museum collections. This example was collected on the Nullarbor Plain in 1920 by F.C. Savage. 290 mm. A46251

MIDDLE RIGHT:

This is perhaps the smallest boomerang known. Barely 50 millimetres from tip to tip, this tiny boomerang was made in 1895 for an Aboriginal child at Killalpaninna, the isolated Lutheran mission on the Cooper Creek, east of Lake Eyre. The boomerang was probably not intended to be thrown, but held as a toy by an infant. 50 mm. A26363

# A BOOMERANG TOUR OF AUSTRALIA

The variation in size, form and decoration of Australian boomerangs mirrors the social and physical diversity of Aboriginal people across the country. With more than 250 distinct languages spoken, it is not surprising to find a similar range of variation in boomerang types.

Even so, it is difficult to divide Australia into distinct 'boomerang regions'. Australian Aboriginal groups are not clearly distinguishable from one another as Native American tribes are, for example. Moreover, boomerang types alter subtly in form and decoration from region to region. Both non-returning and returning boomerangs were used across a large part of the country. There were many local variations of these and a boomerang maker could 'tune' and reshape his boomerang for several different uses – hunting animals or birds, for sport, or as a weapon. As a general rule, larger and heavier boomerangs tended to be used by Aboriginal people of the inland plains and deserts;

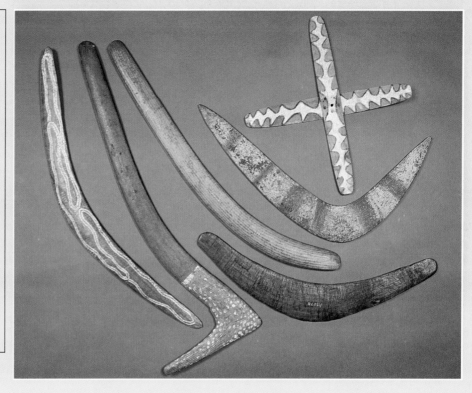

**The diversity of Australian boomerangs.**

RIGHT TO LEFT:

A north Queensland cross-boomerang painted with shark design, a fluted and painted fighting boomerang from north-west Australia, a fluted and ochred Central Australian hunting boomerang, a south-eastern South Australian hunting boomerang, a Central Australian hooked fighting boomerang, a hunting and fighting boomerang from the Cooper Creek region, with infilled pipeclay designs. A42236; A21530; A5407; A5278; A61640; A5574

shorter and lighter boomerangs were used by groups from the higher country and coastal areas. Boomerangs from coastal areas tended to be undecorated with red ochre or carving; the reverse often applied to the inland regions.

Returning boomerangs were rarely used in a broad region roughly corresponding to the Northern Territory and the Lake Eyre basin. They were more commonly used in the south-eastern and south-western parts of the country.

Tasmanian Aboriginal people did not make or use boomerangs at the time of European contact. They may have used them centuries ago, perhaps before the land-bridge to the island was flooded, about 10,000 years ago.

Boomerangs were not thrown in a large part of the Western Desert and in much of far northern Australia but were sometimes traded into these regions as ritual objects.

At the time of European arrival in Australia many of the Aboriginal languages had separate terms for the different types of boomerang found in their regions. The word 'boomerang' became widely used by Europeans, but actually derives from the term *bumariny*, used by Aboriginal speakers of the Dharug language in the Georges River area, south of Sydney. In fact, if Europeans had adopted the term most widely used across Aboriginal Australia, the boomerang would be known today as the 'karli'.

# Kimberley

This rugged region, with its tropical summer storms, woodland vegetation and galleries of rock art, is bordered on its southern and eastern margins by the desert. Five distinct Aboriginal language groups occupy the Kimberley, speaking more than 25 dialects. Not surprisingly, there are several types of Kimberley boomerangs, reflecting local, as well as wider regional influences. Generally, boomerangs of this region are sharply angled, thin, broad-bladed, and often have pointed ends. In former times these boomerangs were often incised with parallel grooves, sometimes with additional decoration consisting of painted bands.

Boomerangs from the coastal regions are distinctive as one arm is often longer than the other and each arm narrows from a wide angle to a point. Examples of this are the remarkable fishing boomerangs of the Broome and Beagle Bay regions.

With strong cultural links to the Western Desert, variations on the Central Australian hunting boomerang also appear in the Kimberley. Hooked boomerangs from the Tennant Creek region were also traded this far west.

Historical records suggest that returning boomerangs were also used in the Kimberley.

Here is a sample of the many Kimberley language terms for the boomerang, with the corresponding language group or region in brackets: *beredie* (Karkarakala), *djeb* (Nyul Nyul), *jarradain lanjee, jarrangur lanjee, karrkarrbeean lanjee, koolmee lanjee, koorilee lanjee, wallagin lanjee, yeelberding lanjee, yeergellee lanjee* (Broome area).

TOP:

As a general rule, boomerangs made by the Aboriginal people of coastal regions around Australia tended to be unochred and undecorated with carving. This hunting boomerang was collected from coastal Kimberley people by pearling captain H.J. Hilliard during the 1890s. 500 mm. A5362

MIDDLE:

A red-ochred hunting boomerang from the inland Kimberley, collected in 1930 by the explorer and surveyor Alfred Canning. The sharp ends are typical of the Kimberley and the thinner, longer form indicates a desert, inland influence. 620 mm. A16998

BOTTOM:

A fine example of a hunting boomerang from the Fitzroy River, almost at the northern limit of boomerang distribution in north Western Australia. The natural history collector, W.P. Dodd, collected this example from an unnamed Fitzroy River man. 540 mm. A835

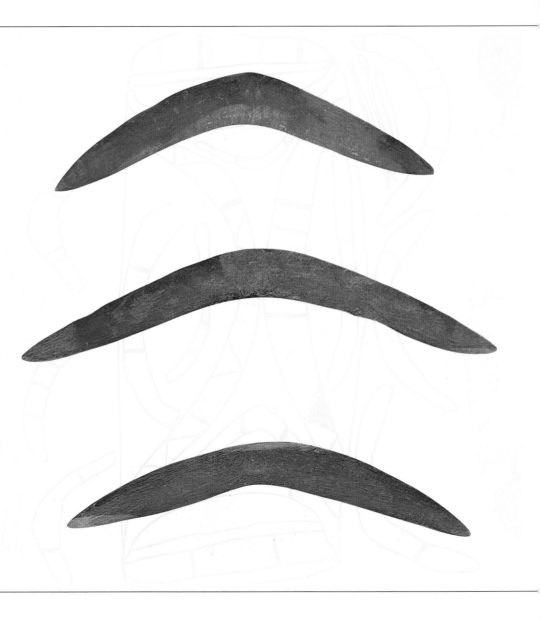

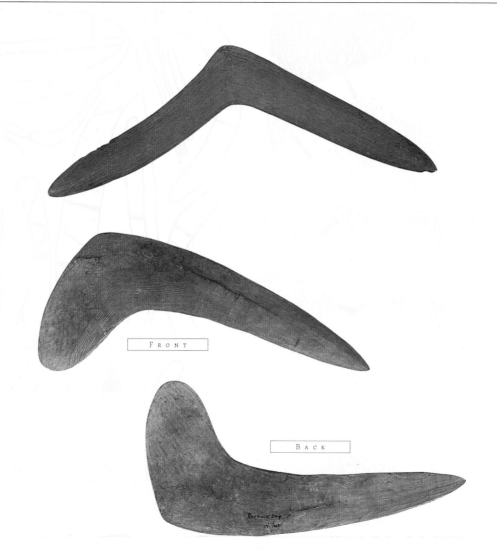

FRONT

BACK

Roebuck Bay
W. Aus

The exaggerated 'jointed' appearance of this boomerang, with one straight and one slightly concave arm, is typical of many from the coastal fringe of Western Australia. The type extended south from the Kimberley, as far as Perth. H.J. Hilliard collected this ochred, lightly-fluted boomerang from Aboriginal people of Roebuck Bay, during the 1890s. 470 mm. A5367

BOTTOM:

Two views of the the distinctive Kimberley fish-killing boomerang, designed to cut through the water and stun large fish. The parallel incisions are unusual, perhaps referring to the maker's totemic affiliation. Very few of these boomerangs are known from museum collections. This example was collected during the 1890s at Roebuck Bay by H.J. Hilliard. 480 mm. A5552

# Central and Northern Australia

Aboriginal men in this region have traditionally made two main types of boomerang, used throughout the open desert plains of Central Australia. Some variations occurred at the southern extent of the region, in and around the MacDonnell Ranges. To the north of the 14th Parallel, where tropical vegetation replaces the grassy plains, boomerangs were used only as musical clap-sticks or as ritual objects.

The simple ochred and longitudinally-fluted boomerang (*karli* or *alye*, etc.) of Central Australia was an essential part of the hunting and tool kit of Aboriginal people

from northern South Australia to Katherine. With painted and ochred decorations it still has a wide use in ceremonial activity. So also does the hooked fighting boomerang (*wirlki*, *irlkwe* etc.), centred traditionally on the Tennant Creek region. This was traded over a wide area of northern Australia, penetrating Arnhem Land, western Queensland, the Kimberley, as well as the southern part of the Northern Territory. Historical records indicate that Aboriginal boys also used returning boomerangs throughout this region.

**TOP:**

A hunting and fighting boomerang belonging to an Arrernte man of the MacDonnell Ranges. Its regular form suggests the Lake Eyre region to the south-east, while the ochred and fluted surface indicates an affinity with the classic hunting boomerangs of the Centre. This boomerang, collected in 1898 by an Alice Springs telegraph station operator, L.H. Griffiths, has also been used as a fire-tending tool. 780 mm. A41346

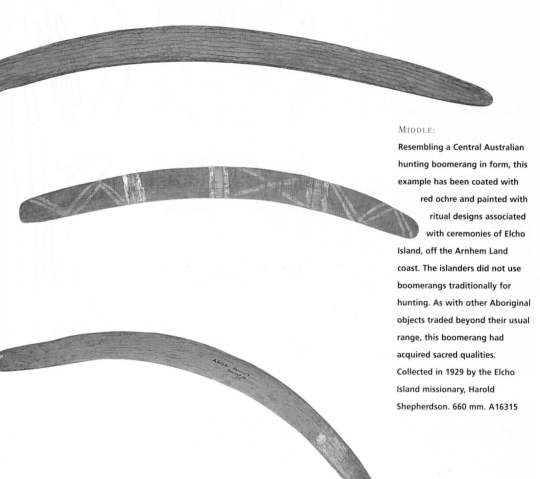

**MIDDLE:**

Resembling a Central Australian hunting boomerang in form, this example has been coated with red ochre and painted with ritual designs associated with ceremonies of Elcho Island, off the Arnhem Land coast. The islanders did not use boomerangs traditionally for hunting. As with other Aboriginal objects traded beyond their usual range, this boomerang had acquired sacred qualities. Collected in 1929 by the Elcho Island missionary, Harold Shepherdson. 660 mm. A16315

**BOTTOM:**

The fluted incisions on the top surface of Central Australian hunting boomerangs are generally not reproduced on the underside. That is the case with this boomerang, collected by the prospector and explorer Charles Chewings. It has been coated with red and yellow ochres for ritual purposes. The glossy patina on the left end confirms it as a right-handed boomerang. 680 mm. A61641

BELOW:

A Daly Waters man decorated for ceremony with body-paint and headgear, holding a boomerang, ca. 1905. The hunting boomerang of Central and Northern Australia was decorated for ceremony in a similar fashion throughout the region, with a single painted design at one end, usually consisting of black motif representing a Dreaming, painted over a background of white dots. (W. Holze, AASAM)

A Central Australian family, photographed during the 1930s. The man is holding a typical 'kit' of tools and weapons – boomerang, spearthrower and shield. Other weapons and the woman's digging stick lie at their feet. (N.B. Tindale, AASAM)

TOP:

The classic Central Australian hunting boomerang, carved with parallel incisions on the upper, convex side and

coated with red ochre as a preservative. The latest scientific research suggests that the rippled incisions may enhance the airfoil capability of the boomerang, in much the same way as the dimples on a golf-ball. A telegraph station operator, J. McKay, collected this boomerang during 1891 at Barrow Creek in Kaytej country. 720 mm. A5407

BOTTOM:

A well-used example of the 'number 7', or hooked, fighting boomerang, used and traded across a large part of north-central Australia. The centre of manufacture is in the Tennant Creek and Tanami Desert regions, associated with the Warlpiri and Warumungu people. The Warlpiri term for this boomerang, *wirlki*, means 'jawbone' – a reference to its general outline. The hook itself is described as *langa*, the 'ear'.

The tiny notch on the top left side marks the point of departure from the hunting boomerang, which is otherwise identical. Made from the junction between a tree trunk and root, the hooked boomerang is stronger than it looks – a lethal fighting weapon. These boomerangs were also used for hunting birds, thrown into flocks of parrots with devastating effect. An Anmatyerre man traded this boomerang to Norman Tindale at Hamilton Downs in 1931. 630 mm. A15766

# Western Australia

This vast area is home to several distinct Aboriginal cultures, from the desert inland, the rugged Pilbara Range, to the well-watered south-west. Despite these cultural differences, and the immensity of the region, the main boomerang types vary only slightly. Western Australian boomerangs are generally lighter and thinner than those of eastern Australia. They also have a more open angle.

The most common type of boomerang, used especially among the main river systems and coastal areas, was an undecorated, thin blade with rounded ends, usually symmetrically shaped. This had a wide distribution, from Roebourne to the southern ocean, and to the South Australian border. Another form has an unusual concavity to one wing's outer edge and sharpened ends. This form was used mainly in the southern part of the state, from Geraldton eastward to Eucla. Both forms included returning examples, particularly in the south-western area. The Central Australian hunting boomerang and the hooked boomerang also penetrated into this region.

TOP:

A Nyangumarta man, Minggu, made this red-ochred hunting boomerang in 1953, at the Eighty Mile Beach, south of Broome, Western Australia. The sharp ends and broad, flattened form is typical of boomerangs from the northern, coastal parts of Western Australia. The anthropologist Norman Tindale recorded the boomerang's name as *jirkili*. 560 mm. A45207

MIDDLE:

A plain, undecorated hunting boomerang, typical of the western districts of Western Australia, collected in 1904 by W.B. Sanders, a station overseer at Nanutarra in the Ashburton River region. 610 mm. A39409

BOTTOM:

In an 1890 letter to the South Australian Museum, the collector of this boomerang, P. St. Barbe Ayliffe, observed that the Aboriginal people of the Gascoyne River 'still use their own [stone] implements for making their weapons which they carve a good deal'. Ayliffe traded goods for this red-ochred hunting boomerang and other artefacts. The boomerang's slim form suggests a connection with the Central Australian hunting boomerang of the desert to the east. 620 mm. A5324

TOP:

Variations on this unusual boomerang type, with one straight arm and the other with a concave twist, were found throughout coastal Western Australia. The type apparently reached its most extreme form in the south-western region of the Lyons River, north of Perth. A range of modern competition boomerangs also use this 'hook' design. This boomerang was probably collected by station overseer G.H. Birt around 1900. 630 mm. A5477

MIDDLE:

This boomerang, thin, light, and open-bladed with sharp ends, was probably used for hunting and fighting. It was collected in about 1900 in the Northam-Perth region by Walter Howchin, an Adelaide geologist with a strong interest in Aboriginal archaeology. 640 mm. A26688

BOTTOM:

The unusual 'jointed' design of this long boomerang is found throughout the goldfields and south-western regions of Western Australia. The single rounded handle is a notable feature. The surface carvings are similar to those found on spearthrowers and carved shields in the region. Telegraph station operator A.C. Clayer collected this boomerang at Eucla, near the South Australian border, prior to 1914. 900 mm. A2061

# Lake Eyre Basin and Darling River

This region includes the driest part of Australia, traversed by river systems which periodically flood from rains which may fall hundreds of kilometres away. In pre-European times, Aboriginal people used these river systems as havens, travelling again as unpredictable rains brought life to the desert country.

Aboriginal men of this region, extending across much of eastern Central Australia, carved distinctively heavy boomerangs, using them for hunting and fighting. These boomerangs were intricately incised, and the detailed carvings were often highlighted with white pipeclay. The reliance on boomerangs in this region may reflect the fact that spears and spearthrowers were rarely used.

Even the smallest boomerangs in this region were considerably longer and heavier than those of other regions. Hunters threw these smaller boomerangs end over end, so that they cartwheeled towards an enemy or prey. They rarely used small or light boomerangs, and returning boomerangs are known only from mythology. Men used the largest boomerangs (up to two metres in length) as swords or staves in hand-to-hand combat only. These boomerangs are the longest in Aboriginal Australia.

Aboriginal people of this region traded their boomerangs widely – east into New South Wales and Queensland, and to the west of Lake Eyre as far as the MacDonnell Ranges.

The relatively homogeneous nature of Aboriginal material culture across this region seems to have resulted in a relatively restricted range of language terms for the boomerang. Here is a sample, with corresponding language group or region in brackets: *karra* (Peake), *keera* (Warburton River), *kirra* (Diyari), *murrawirrie* (Wangkangurru), *ngamiringa* (Lake Eyre), *wana* (Torowotto), *yarrakoodakoodari* (Cooper Creek).

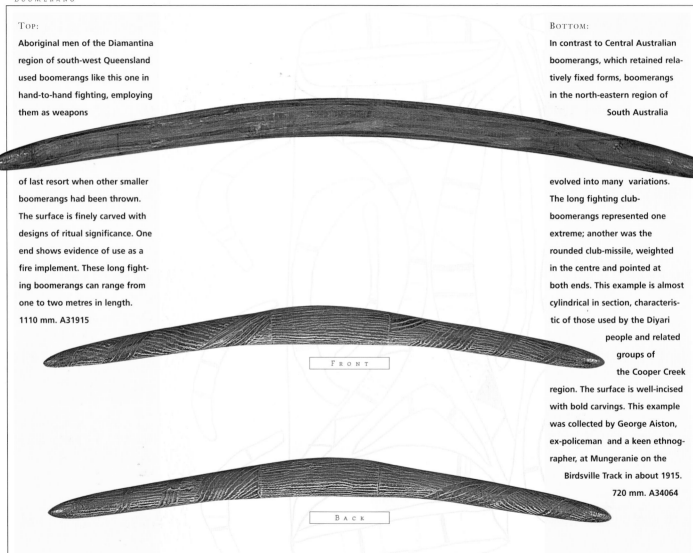

TOP:

Aboriginal men of the Diamantina region of south-west Queensland used boomerangs like this one in hand-to-hand fighting, employing them as weapons of last resort when other smaller boomerangs had been thrown. The surface is finely carved with designs of ritual significance. One end shows evidence of use as a fire implement. These long fighting boomerangs can range from one to two metres in length. 1110 mm. A31915

BOTTOM:

In contrast to Central Australian boomerangs, which retained relatively fixed forms, boomerangs in the north-eastern region of South Australia evolved into many variations. The long fighting club-boomerangs represented one extreme; another was the rounded club-missile, weighted in the centre and pointed at both ends. This example is almost cylindrical in section, characteristic of those used by the Diyari people and related groups of the Cooper Creek region. The surface is well-incised with bold carvings. This example was collected by George Aiston, ex-policeman and a keen ethnographer, at Mungeranie on the Birdsville Track in about 1915. 720 mm. A34064

FRONT

BACK

TOP:

Here the carver has achieved a fluid symmetry with these sinuous designs highlighted with pipeclay. The designs may represent the travels of a Dreaming Ancestor or the course of a river system. The 'pinched' ends suggest that this boomerang originated in the western side of the Lake Eyre basin, in New South Wales or southern Queensland. 720 mm. A5575

BOTTOM:

These hooked boomerangs present a problem for ethnographers – there is no evidence of them being used for fighting or hunting in the Cooper Creek region. In many cases the hook appears to have served only a decorative purpose. Such boomerangs are likely to have been used in ceremonies, particularly as they are often painted, or decorated with incised patterns as on this example. The South Australian Museum director, Edward Stirling, purchased this boomerang in 1899 from Aboriginal people camped at Cowarie Station, north of Lake Eyre. 790 mm. A5528

# Central and Eastern Queensland

In this region the great variety of Aboriginal language groups is reflected in a multiplicity of language terms for the boomerang. Here is a sample: *barakadan* (Moreton Bay), *barengun* (Stradbroke Island), *bibapooro* (Boulia), *buegarrah* (Ingham), *burrong* (Herbert River), *byerla* (Yelina), *dhugarli* (Wakaya), *jaguy* (Yidiny), *juluwarr* (Lardil), *kulgai* (Hughenden River), *mangany* (Wanyurr), *nyaral* (Tully River), *torooroo* (Kalkadoon), *winche* (Princess Charlotte Bay), *wolloomba* (Kalkadoon), *wongal* (Halifax Bay), *wongala* (Mackay), *yalkabray* (Cloncurry), *yintyoor gidyar* (Yidiny).

OPPOSITE PAGE:

Performers in the Mudlunga ceremony, a non-secret cult ceremony which travelled through a large part of eastern and Central Australia from the 1890s to the 1930s. This photograph shows men of the Guwa group, near Winton, Queensland, in 1938. Boomerangs were integral elements in the performance.

(N.B.Tindale, AASAM)

This area encompasses a wide range of Aboriginal cultural regions, from the relatively sedentary and isolated rainforest people, to coastal fishing communities and the inland plains, where more mobile groups relied on hunting to supplement a diet of ground grass-seed flour. It is difficult to generalise about the boomerangs used across the region, beyond observing that they are relatively long, usually around 90 centimetres, and tend towards a crescent shape. They are generally unochred, with sometimes only a lightly-incised decoration. Regional differences consist of pointed or round ends and varying degrees of curvature. Returning boomerangs are known throughout the region, particularly nearer the coast.

The unique form of Australian cross-boomerang was traditionally found at the northern end of this area, concentrated in the Cairns rainforest region. This type, often decorated with painted designs, was used in games and occasionally decorated for ceremonial purposes. One isolated record, from northern New South Wales, suggests that the cross-boomerang was also used as a returning boomerang for hunting waterbirds.

TOP:

Mornington and Bentinck Islands provide exceptions to the general lack of boomerangs along Australia's northern coast. The relevant influence here is from the Gulf country to the south. Mick Charles, a Janggal man, made this example, red-ochred and decorated in typical fashion, during 1960. 480 mm. A53210

BOTTOM:

The crescent shape and sharp ends indicate an affinity with a region extending south into north-eastern New South Wales. Note the roughened hand-grip. This boomerang was collected during the 1890s by Clement Wragge from an unknown Aboriginal man at the south-central Queensland railway town of Alpha. 690 mm. A5384

MIDDLE:

A light boomerang collected by Clement Wragge during the 1890s at Tewantin, near the present-day resort town of Noosa. This may have been used by Aboriginal people for hunting birds, and probably had a returning capacity. 590 mm. A5380

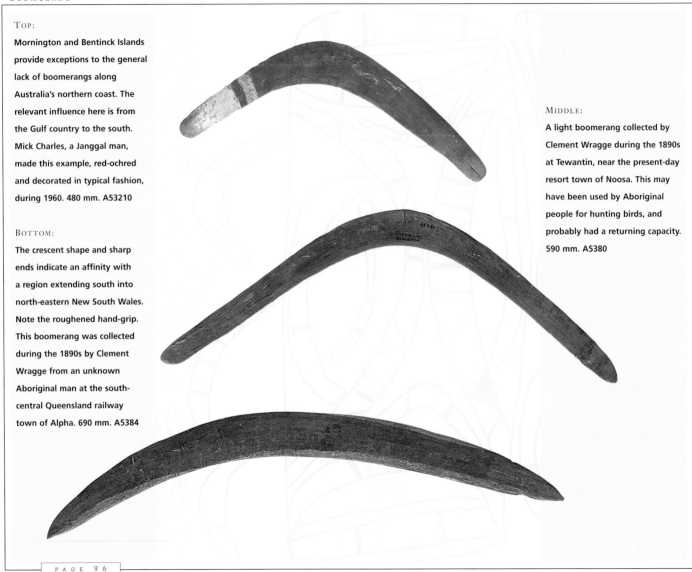

TOP:

An ochred cross-boomerang, collected in 1907 from rainforest Aboriginal people near Cairns by missionary E.R. Gribble. The two arms are bound together with cane. The cross-boomerang's distribution was relatively limited, and was confined mainly to the Cairns region. This example was probably used in games and competitions. The cross-boomerang was also painted with totemic designs and featured in Aboriginal ceremonies of the region. 440 mm. A2860

BOTTOM:

A thin and light boomerang, possibly made of mangrove wood. Aboriginal men used these boomerangs, which probably had a returning capacity, for hunting birds. Clement Wragge collected this boomerang during the 1890s from an Aboriginal man of the Moreton Bay district, close to the present site of Brisbane. The carving at the left end may have been incised as a hand-grip, suggesting that this was a left-hander's boomerang. 550 mm. A32055

MIDDLE:

A fighting boomerang known as *loangal* by the Buluwandji people of the Kuranda area in north-eastern Queensland. This was collected in 1938 by Norman Tindale, who recorded that the boomerang was capable of killing an opponent. 440 mm. A27409

BACK

FRONT

# South-eastern Australia

In this region, which takes in southern New South Wales, Victoria and south-eastern South Australia, Aboriginal people used two main boomerang types – fighting or hunting boomerangs and smaller returning boomerangs. Both forms are usually undecorated by incisions or ochre.

In general, the larger, heavier boomerangs were used by Aboriginal groups of the inland plains, to the west of the Great Dividing Range, while the lighter and smaller boomerangs tended to be used by coastal or riverine groups, or those in mountainous regions. In this relatively well-watered and resource-rich region, Aboriginal people lived in more populous communities and were less nomadic than inland people. One consequence was that they relied upon a greater number of specialised artefacts. Boomerangs were not the all-purpose tools of desert people.

Fighting or hunting boomerangs, up to 90 centimetres long, were thrown through the air or cartwheeled along the ground. Lighter returning boomerangs with thin, broad blades and a sharp 'elbow' were more common, used for hunting water-birds on lakes and waterways. In parts of Victoria Aboriginal hunters used returning boomerangs made of bark for this purpose.

The returning boomerang of this region, the first to be heavily affected by British settlement, contributed to the stereotype of the Aboriginal hunter that endures today.

kertum (Wimmera), ketum-ketum (Mount Gambier), kowil (MacLeay River), mulla murrale (Warrego River), paang geetch (Kuurn kopan noot), panketyi (Ngarrindjeri), pungo gnapp (Chaap wurrong), wangin (Southern Gippsland), wunya (MurrayGoulburn junction), wurangaing (Wodi-wodi).

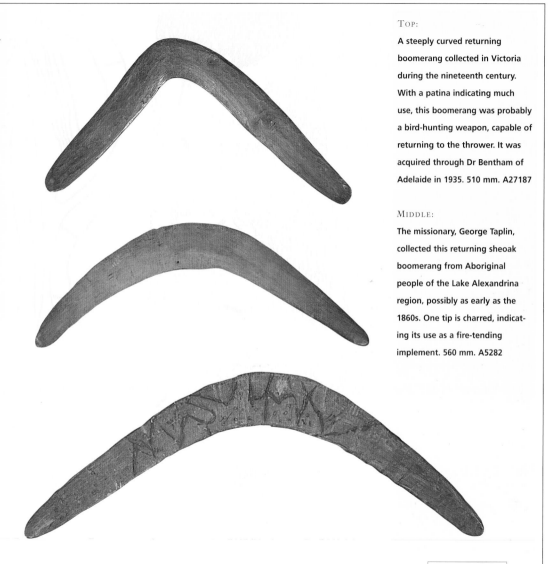

TOP:

A steeply curved returning boomerang collected in Victoria during the nineteenth century. With a patina indicating much use, this boomerang was probably a bird-hunting weapon, capable of returning to the thrower. It was acquired through Dr Bentham of Adelaide in 1935. 510 mm. A27187

MIDDLE:

The missionary, George Taplin, collected this returning sheoak boomerang from Aboriginal people of the Lake Alexandrina region, possibly as early as the 1860s. One tip is charred, indicating its use as a fire-tending implement. 560 mm. A5282

BOTTOM:

A returning boomerang of the Meningie region, near Lake Alexandrina. The collector, Constable Marshall, noted that Aboriginal people of the region no longer used boomerangs by 1890, but he was able to commission a set of weapons from an old man. The man added the decorations, which were branded on with hot wire. 640 mm. A35322

TOP:

The naturalist Charles Daley collected this hunting boomerang from Aboriginal people of south-central New South Wales, probably during the 1890s. This is an intermediate type between the heavy boomerangs of the Lake Eyre Basin and the lighter, more angular boomerangs of south-eastern Australia. 700 mm. A36484

MIDDLE:

The cross-hatched decoration and rounded form of this hunting boomerang suggest that it originated in New South Wales. It was collected prior to 1911. 430 mm. A5299

BOTTOM:

Still a boomerang in general outline and its plano-convex form, this example is closer to the so-called 'lil-lil' clubs of New South Wales. Like many of those clubs, the head of this example is carved with the zig-zag patterning distinctive to south-eastern Australia. This was collected during the 1890s by the station overseer G.H. Birt at Sturt's Meadow in western New South Wales. 710 mm. A5543

# Gawler Ranges and Flinders Ranges

Despite great variety in the landscape – from rolling hills and open plains to rocky gorges and sandy desert – this broad region embraced a single Aboriginal language group, with dialectal differences. This uniformity is mirrored in the gradual shift in boomerang types found here, from the Gawler to the Flinders Ranges. Most boomerangs were of middle size and weight, about 50 centimetres in length. These were used for hunting and fighting. Returning boomerangs were known in this region, and large boomerangs were used for hand-to-hand combat.

After European arrival boomerangs were often carved with figurative designs, sometimes depicting hunting scenes or totemic animals. Particularly fine work was produced in the Flinders Ranges during the 1930s and 1940s. A geometric style was developed at the western end of the Gawler Ranges near Tarcoola, and was subsequently adopted by Aboriginal people of the Yalata region for sale to tourists.

The continuity of boomerang types across this region appears to reflect linguistic similarities between the Wirangu, Parnkala, Flinders Ranges and Lake Eyre groups.

The linguistic uniformity of this region is reflected in the small number of Aboriginal language terms for the boomerang. Here is a selection, with the corresponding language group or region in brackets: *coohah* (Fowlers Bay), *kali* (Wirangu), *wadnana* (Parnkala), *wadna* (Adnyamathanha, Ngadjuri, Narrunga), *watnah* (Venus Bay), *wonna* (Melrose), *woodna* (Crystal Brook).

TOP:

Purchased at Yalata on South Australia's west coast in 1965, the slim form of this long boomerang reflects an influence from the local region and the Gawler Ranges. The snake designs may refer to one of the major Dreamings traversing the Nullarbor Plain. The carver has left the snakes' bodies blank, surrounding them with incised patterns, highlighted with pipeclay. 1020 mm. A57228

MIDDLE:

This style of boomerang, carved in an elongated crescent, was found along the west coast of South Australia and Eyre Peninsula. The carvings have been branded on with a hot metal implement. This boomerang was collected in 1901 by the explorer R.T. Maurice from Aboriginal people living at Fowlers Bay. 1030 mm. A5665

BOTTOM:

The central panel of incised design on this carved boomerang is similar to those of the Lake Eyre region. Trading and ceremonial links explain this connection. The geometric carvings on this finely-balanced boomerang from Yardea in the Gawler Ranges probably relate to the maker's totem or Dreaming affiliation. 780 mm. A32042

BOTTOM:

In its general form this boomerang resembles those traditionally made and used in the Flinders Ranges. The carvings represent the high point of tourist art for the region, and were made by older, initiated men for whom the apparently secular designs carried considerable meaning. The central figure of the eagle, for example, is a major Dreaming figure associated with much of the Flinders Ranges landscape and traditions. The fight of the snake and lizard represents another epic Dreaming battle. The 'pecked' background design surrounds the figures, which were soaked in water to emerge in relief, then singed black. This boomerang is attributed to Henry Wilton and Ted Coulthard, two renowned Adnyamathanha carvers. It was made at Nepabunna in about 1950. 470 mm. A41757

TOP RIGHT:

This hunting boomerang was collected during the 1880s from Adnyamathanha people in the Mount Serle–Myrtle Springs area of the Flinders Ranges. Slightly ochred, the plain surface contrasts with the more elaborate carved boomerangs from the Flinders Ranges which were made in response to the European tourist market after the 1920s. 680 mm. A51168

# BOOMERANGABILIA

If any single object has crossed the boundaries between indigenous and western culture it is the boomerang. During the two centuries since its discovery by Europeans, the boomerang has flown into many different spheres, appearing in the form of souvenirs, kitsch ornaments, advertising graphics, military emblems and civic design. Even the shape of Australia's Parliament House in Canberra is modelled on two boomerangs.

Two Australian icons: the laughing jackass or kookaburra, perched on a boomerang. Australia Day badge, 1918 – a high point for emerging Australian nationalism. Private collections.

This process of 'appropriation' of the boomerang did much to trivialise Aboriginal culture at a time when Europeans had little appreciation of the religious, land-based nature of Aboriginal society.

Retail displays of souvenir boomerangs are common in airport shops across Australia in the 1990s. (AASAM)

# European Fascination with the Boomerang

Most people would assume this man is Aboriginal because he is holding a boomerang, notwithstanding the fact that the 'boomerang' is not of Australian origin. This late nineteenth-century studio photograph was probably produced for the emerging postcard trade. (AASAM)

When it reached Australia in 1788, the First Fleet included several Europeans who observed and recorded Aboriginal customs and artefacts in the region of Sydney. While at least three accounts documented the use of non-returning boomerangs, describing these as 'wooden swords', there was no mention of returning boomerangs.

It was not until late 1802 that the first account of these appeared in the journal of Francis Louis Barrallier, a French-born ensign in the New South Wales Corps. His record of the artefact was made some distance inland from Sydney:

*The natives of this part of the country make use of a weapon which is not employed by, and is even unknown to, the natives of Sydney. It is composed of a piece of wood in the form of a half circle which they make as sharp as a sabre on both edges, and pointed at each end. They throw it on the ground or in the air, making it revolve on itself, and with such a velocity that one cannot see it returning towards the ground; only the whizzing of it is heard.*
(Quoted in Smith 1992: 67-68)

Within two years of Barrallier's observation, Aboriginal people of the Sydney region were using the returning boomerang. The artefact was probably taken there by Aboriginal people attracted to the strange features of the new settlement.

Europeans soon had the opportunity to see the returning boomerang being demonstrated in earnest by Bungaree, the best known of the Sydney Aboriginal people, originally from the Broken Bay region.

*. . . the white spectators were justly astonished at the dexterity and incredible force with which a bent, edged waddy resembling slightly a Turkish scyemetar was thrown by Bungary, a native distinguished by his remarkable courtesy. The weapon, thrown at 20 or 30 yards distance, twirled round in the air with astonishing velocity, and alighting on the right arm of one of his opponents, actually rebounded to a distance not less than 70 or 80 yards, leaving a horrible contusion behind, and exciting universal admiration.* (Quoted in Smith 1992: 67)

**Men of the Port Stephens area, drawn by George French Angas during 1845. By this time, more than fifty years after the First Fleet, Aboriginal people were living at the fringes of European towns, earning money by giving boomerang-throwing demonstrations. (AASAM)**

Within a few years, the scientific curiosity of European observers was fully aroused. Barron Field described the boomerang as:

*a short crested weapon which the natives of Port Jackson project with accurate aim into a rotary motion, which gives a precalculated bias to its forcible fall.* (The Australian National Dictionary, 1988)

Boomerangs soon caught the imagination of writers in Europe. During the 1830s some boomerangs found their way to Dublin and a boomerang-throwing craze took off rapidly. University students there and at Oxford and Cambridge were especially taken with the new fad.

New South Wales explorer, politician and inventor Sir Thomas Mitchell attempted to apply the principle of the boomerang to the construction of a ship's propeller. He outlined his theories in an 1851 lecture (*Sydney Morning Herald,* 11 January 1851) and published on the subject in 1852 (Mitchell 1852).

The origin of the boomerang soon became a controversial subject. Some theorists explained the boomerang's presence in Australia by suggesting that Ancient Egyptians had taken it there. These 'diffusionists' were met by 'social evolutionists' who argued that independent Australian invention of the boomerang proved that Aboriginal people were gradually evolving towards 'civilisation'.

From the late nineteenth century the boomerang became an instant marker of Aboriginal authenticity for Europeans interested in the 'primitive' and the exotic. Studio photographs of Aboriginal people often included a boomerang as a prop, regardless of its relevance.

This fascination with the boomerang tells us more about the readiness of European observers to categorise and rank other cultures than it tells us about Aboriginal culture itself.

Aboriginal boomerangs – and people – as museum exhibits, 1929. A Wangkangurru man, Jack Noorywauka and an Arrrernte man, Stan Loycurrie, photographed with ethnographer George Aiston at the 'Outback' exhibition organised by the National Museum of Victoria, Melbourne. (*Chronicle*, 29 August 1929)

# Military and Patriotic Emblems

Three qualities combined to make the boomerang a powerful military and patriotic symbol: its status as a weapon, its identification with the Australian nation, and its capacity to return.

The boomerang was used as a military and patriotic emblem during the first world war. This association persists today – in the 1990s the Australian contingent of the United Nations peace-keeping force in Cambodia incorporated the boomerang into their unofficial insignia.

Badges and pins incorporating the boomerang motif, early twentieth century. The boomerang symbol had a special resonance for servicemen and servicewomen whose return was anticipated by those at home.

(Private collections)

This boomerang was sent to a serviceman's mother as a gift from the Alice Springs area. An Aboriginal carver probably made the boomerang and sold it as a 'blank', to be decorated by a soldier with artistic flair.

# The Boomerang in the Suburbs

RIGHT:

The boomerang as kitsch. This ashtray with an Aboriginal figure seated on crossed boomerangs did nothing to engender respect or understanding of Aboriginal culture during the 1950s.

(Private collection)

The boomerang found a place in the homes of middle Australia well before Aboriginal art became widely accepted. In fact, from the turn of this century an entire range of ephemeral household items incorporated the boomerang shape. The cheap and disposable nature of these items – ashtrays, plates, tablecloths, hair-brushes and vases – tells us something of the way Aboriginal culture was regarded within Australian society until recently.

The boomerang became a popular symbol of the social connections which may exist between individuals – well suited to the convivial occasions of eating, drinking and smoking.

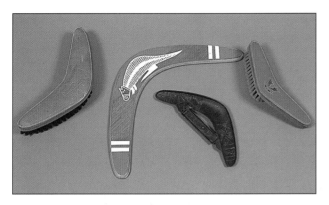

A Mannum Rowing Club singlet, adorned with boomerang insignia. (D. Lindner)

In the suburbs of the 1950s and 1960s the 'cocktail hour' was the setting, with boomerang-shaped bottle openers, and the symbol appeared on glassware, mats, and drink coasters. It is ironic that the main public locations for these activities – pubs and licensed restaurants – were barred to Aboriginal people until 1967.

## Clubs and Crests

With its bold and strong outline, the boomerang has often been adopted as an emblem by various sporting clubs – even a motorcycle club. During the 1980s, the first Aboriginal soccer club to tour internationally was named 'The Boomerangs'. The boomerang has also been incorporated into the crests of organisations and institutions seeking to refer to an Australian context.

The official ANZ Bank sponsor's matchbox released for the 1984 Olympic Games.

# A Boomerang Obsession

**Tin containing the 'Boomerang' brand harmonica, made by the Albert family, Sydney.**

Every so often the boomerang possesses its owner! The Albert family of Sydney have been this country's most successful publisher of sheet music for most of this century. They published the Boomerang Songster series, manufactured the Boomerang Harmonica, and had Boomerang House as their King Street, Sydney, headquarters. In 1926 Frank Albert built Australia's finest example of an art deco home and called it 'Boomerang'. It includes a terrazzo boomerang set into the floor of the swimming pool.

## Mementos and Souvenirs

**'Greetings from Ballarat, 1918'. An evocative plaster kookaburra and boomerang combination.**

**(Private collection)**

The returning boomerang has been used as a symbol of personal reminder for many decades. As well as this, the boomerang's flight has represented the links between individuals across distances and through time. For most of this century, the boomerang has been the ideal tourist souvenir, providing overseas and Australian travellers with a reminder of their journeys, as well as their destinations. In exploring opportunities for tourist art, Aboriginal people themselves have often promoted this role for the boomerang.

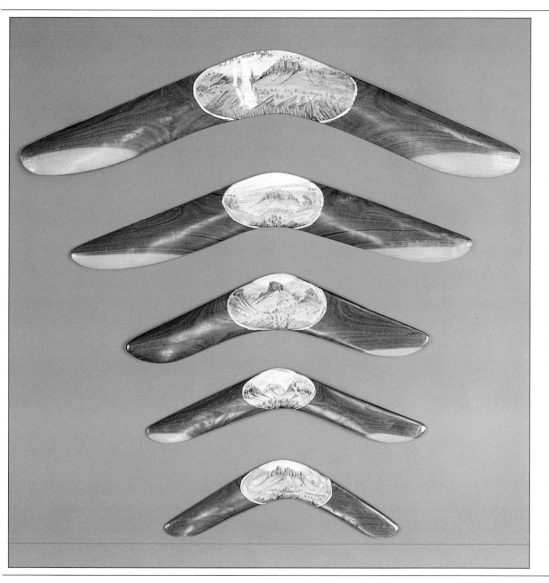

A set of five boomerangs with Central Australian landscapes, thought to have been painted by the famous Arrernte artist, Albert Namatjira. This set was made for the tourist trade which began to influence Aboriginal art production in Central Australia after the 1940s. (Private collection)

ABOVE AND BELOW:

These small boomerang fridge-magnets are made by Aboriginal people of Alice Springs during the 1990s and are decorated with Dreaming designs. Peter Marshall's (above) shows a 'Men's Ceremony' design; Brenda Dixon's (below) depicts the 'Grevillea Honey Dreaming'. (P. Jones)

# Boomerangs in Advertising

A shop dispenser for 'Boomerang' cigarette papers, probably dating from the 1920s.

(Private collection)

The boomerang was a boon to the Australian advertising industry which emerged during the late nineteenth century. 'Boomerang' brandy, butter, cigarette papers, flour, etc all became instantly recognisable products. Beyond this, of course, was the image of a product returning to the customer, or the customer to the product – recurrent themes that sustain the advertising industry.

Catches the Germ as well as the Fly

Sanitary and Non-Poisonous

BOOMERANG FLY-PAPER

MANUFACTURED IN AUSTRALIA

ULLADULLA REFRIGERATING BUTTER Co. LTD. N.S.W.

TRADE MARK

BOOMERANG BRAND

56 lbs Nett

The boomerang was soon appropriated as a symbol by Europeans, and became used in advertising from the 1860s onward. These are just a few of the many boomerang advertisements dating from the late nineteenth century. (Cozzolino 1980)

BOOMERANG

JOSHUA'S "BOOMERANG" Australian Brandy

THE BOOMERANG

56 lbs NET

TRADE MARK

BOOMERANG

YINNAR BUTTER FACTORY

VICTORIA AUSTRALIA

THE BOOMERANG BRAND

## The Travelling Boomerang

The boomerang has had particular appeal for the Australian travel industry. It has been a feature of Australian motel advertising ('please come back soon') and bus companies ('we'll bring you home safely') for several decades.

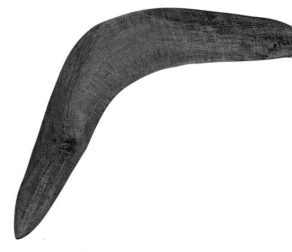

The larger photographs on these two pages show postcards which neatly depict the boomerang's role in the travel industry. (Qantas Historical Archives; Orient Line)

OPPOSITE PAGE, BOTTOM:
The Australian astronaut, Andrew Thomas, took this boomerang into orbit during his 1996 *Endeavour* space shuttle mission. The boomerang from south-eastern Australia is part of the South Australian Museum's collection.

there's less to pay the boomerang way

ORIENT LINE

**BOOMERANG TRIPS**

ENGLAND-AUSTRALIA ✦ AUSTRALIA-ENGLAND

An advertising sign outside the 'Boomerang Motel', Rankins Springs, New South Wales. Photographed at night by the proprietor, M.J. Parks.

1960s tourist road-map of the Northern Territory, incorporating silhouettes of an Aboriginal man and a boomerang. (P. Jones)

# Novelty Boomerangs

TOP RIGHT:

This returning boomerang, illuminated with built-in globes, was thrown over the Berlin Wall at night from West Berlin, on 27 August 1988. (B. Ruhe)

BOTTOM (LEFT TO RIGHT):

**Kangaroo.** By David Ratliff, Magee, Mississippi.

**Woman.** By George Reitbauer, West Chester, Pennsylvania.

**Rabbit.** By Dominique Pouillet of Paris.

As boomerangs have flown further and further from Aboriginal culture, they have taken on many new meanings and associations. The returning boomerang has been combined with other cultural symbols, objects and clichés – such as Bugs Bunny, the kangaroo and the platypus, Mick's hat in the movie *Crocodile Dundee*, a tennis racket or a pair of thongs. Enthusiasts have made their boomerangs perform peculiar feats – such as fly around the South Pole, travel in a jumbo jet over the International Date Line, or jump over the Berlin Wall and back.

# The Modern Returning Boomerang

The commercially produced modern returning boomerang is rarely Aboriginal-made and is often manufactured overseas. It is usually made of plywood, plastic or cardboard and is designed as a safe toy. Australian returning boomerangs are made primarily with tourists in mind, but often Aboriginal Australians are barely mentioned in the accompanying instructions.

This polystyrene tri-blade returning boomerang has a range of twelve metres. It was made by Sam Blight of 'Rangs', Perth, Western Australia (T. Bailey)

ABOVE:

The Darnell Boomerang, developed during the 1980s. 'Its revolutionary design makes it highly visible, easy to tune, and indestructible.' - Chet Snouffler, 1985 World Boomerang Champion. (B.Ruhe collection)

# An International Sport

**Poster advertising the first annual Smithsonian Boomerang Throwing Tournament, 1979. This highly successful event, organised by Benjamin Ruhe and held at the Washington D.C. Mall, signalled the dawn of the modern era of boomerang-throwing as an international sport and hobby. (AASAM)**

There are now hundreds of boomerang-throwing clubs around the world. The sport was almost exclusively Australian until Ben Ruhe inaugurated the annual Smithsonian Boomerang Throwing Tournament in Washington D.C. during 1979. Within two decades the sport has spread to many countries, with enthusiasts in countries such as Japan, Finland, India and Africa joining those in Australia, the United States and Europe. Boomerang-throwing is now under consideration as a future Olympic sport.

Tournaments include a range of events, such as fast-catch, juggling, 'doubling' and, of course, the long-distance throw and return. The table opposite gives some current long-distance records among some of the principal competing nations.

**Ross Witherspoon of Melbourne throws a returning boomerang at 5800 metres in Nepal, 1991.**

# Long-distance Records

| COUNTRY | NAME | DISTANCE (metres) | COMPETITION | |
|---|---|---|---|---|
| France | Michel Dufayard | 149.12 | Shrewsbury | 1992 |
| USA | Jim Youngblood | 134.2 | Poolesville | 1989 |
| Germany | Udo Wenning | 122.2 | Sedan | 1993 |
| Switzerland | Lorenz Gubler | 120.72 | Kiel | 1995 |
| Australia | Bob Burwell | 113 | Sydney | 1982 |
| England | Gordon Shuttleworth | 103.5 | Sedan | 1993 |
| Belgium | Daniel Luycx | 101.9 | Troyes | 1994 |
| Holland | Johan Klaase Bos | 101.74 | Kiel | 1995 |
| Bulgaria | Miroslav Ditchev | 82.95 | Kiel | 1995 |
| Sweden | Ola Wahlberg | 81.15 | Kiel | 1995 |
| Italy | M. & P. Crescimbeni | 80 | Chantilly | 1990 |

Commemorative T-shirt logo from the 1988 boomerang-throwing championships in Munster, Germany. (B. Ruhe collection)

BELOW:

Modern competition boomerangs designed by Ted Bailey, a prize-winning American boomerang designer. On the left are 'tri-bladers' used in 'fast-catch' events ( multiple throw/catch sequences). On the right are a selection of boomerangs used in 'maximum-time-aloft' competions.

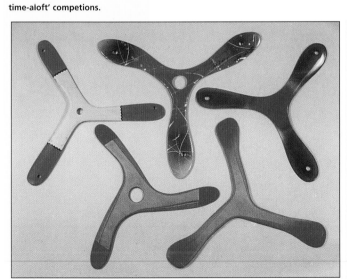

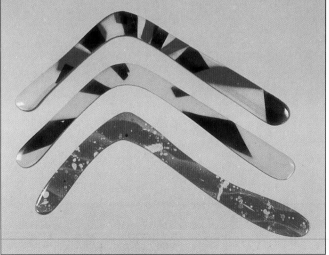

# The Boomerang in Print and on the Internet

With the growth of satirical and critical magazines during the 1860s and 1870s, the boomerang was an obvious choice as a symbol. This magazine, *The Boomerang Serio-Comic*, was 'hurled at passing events' from Sydney during the 1870s.

RIGHT:

*Boomerangs – Echoes of Australia (1996),* an interactive CD-Rom based on the South Australian Museum's collection, is the first multi-media exploration of the boomerang's history and use.

(Dynamic Computer Solutions)

Since it came to the attention of Europeans during the early nineteenth century, the boomerang has attracted a profusion of printed references – from scientific articles and museum labels to poetry and jokes. The bibliography at the end of this book provides a wide sampling of this literature.

*Boomerang News* is an invaluable newsletter and resource for international boomerang followers. It is published by Ted Bailey, P.O.Box 6076, Ann Arbor, MI 48106-6076, United States of America.

More recently, the boomerang has appeared on the world-wide web. Boomerang-throwing associations are active users of the web, advertising competitions and the latest designs. A subject search for 'boomerang' also reveals that the word has entered the language as a term of scientific and advertising jargon, suggesting something which will return, or something to which a consumer will return.

# World Boomerang Clubs and Organizations

## North and South America

Bumerangue Clube do Brasil
Carlos Martini Filho
Caixa Postal 13.074
01.000 Sao Paulo, SP
Brazil

Boomerang Assoc. of Canada
Attn: John Cryderman
136 Thames Street
Chatham N7L 2Y8
Ontario, Canada

Club de Boom de Montreal
Attn: Stephane Marguerite
2114 rue de Chambly
Montreal (QC) H1W 3J4
Quebec, Canada

United States Boomerang
Association
Attn: Chet or Carmen Souffer
P.O. Box 182
Delaware, OH 43015
USA

The World of Boomerangs
Attn: Tom Fitzgerald
1159 Holly River Drive
Florissant, Missouri 63031
USA

## United Kingdom and Europe

Bulgarian Boomerang Club
Attn: Georgi Dimantchev
Hipodruma 139A-A-23
1612 Sofia
Bulgaria

Finnish Boomerang Club
Attn: Harri pietila
Rantamaenkatu 4 as. 18
20300 Turku
Finland

Boomerang Club Dijon
Attn: Didier Bonin
8 Place Centrale
21800 Quetigny
France

Club A. Turck
Attn: Dominique Lambert
155 Allee du paVillon
77 190 Dammarie les lys
France

France Boomerang Assoc.
Attn: Olivier Vouktchevitch
BP 62
91002 Evry Cedex
France

La Perouse Boomerang
Club de France
Attn: Denis LeMaitre
6, Rue des Etats-Generaux
78000 Versailles
France

Bumerang Welt
Attn: Wilhelm Bretfeld
Postfach 3230
22825 Norderstedt
Germany

Deutschen Bumerang Club
Attn: Ulli Wegner
Meller Strasse 59
33613 Bielefeld
Germany

A.B.O. Holland
Attn: Han Paesi
Grote Wittenburgerstraat
45d
1018 KV Amsterdam
Holland

Fed. Italiana Boomerang
Attn: Mario Crescimbeni
C.P. 86
37100 Verona
Italy

Italian Boomerang Club
Attn: Maurizio Saba
Via del Trullo 122
00148 Roma
Italy

Club Di Portivo Fortuna
Fernando Linares
Apartado 856
20080 San Sebastian
Spain

Swedish Boomerang Society
Attn: Ola Wahlberg
Brunnegardsvagen 1
433 32 Partille
Sweden

Swiss Boomerang Fed.
Attn: Thomas Stehrenberger
Tosstahlstrasse 249
8405 Winterthur
Switzerland

British Boomerang Society
Attn: Sean Slade
1 Berkeley Ave.
Mapperley Park
Nottingham NG3 5BU
United Kingdom

## Asia and South Pacific

Japan Boomerang
Association
Nippon Boomerang No Kai
Attn: Yoshinobu Sakimitsu
15-5 Kudan-Kita, 1-Chome
Chiyoda-Ku, Tokyo 102
Japan

Guinobatan Boomerang Club
Attn: Erwin P. Brojan
Guinobatan Post Office
Buinobatan, Albay 4503
Philippines

Champion Australian boomerang competitor Frank Donnellan ('Holder of All Records') promises to 'reveal secrets which have made me an International figure in the Boomerang Throwing World' – on the cover of a 1950s boomerang-throwing publication.

A postcard dating from 1909, depicting Aboriginal boomerang throwers at Lake Tyers Mission, Victoria. (AASAM)

# The Boomerang's Erratic Flight

Since its discovery by Europeans, the boomerang has described a trajectory which has taken it far from its original context within Aboriginal material culture. It has been incorporated within European social theory and popular culture, it has found a place within military symbolism, product advertising, tourist ephemera, and modern and post-modern art. More recently it has become completely dissociated from its Aboriginal origins, as a North American and European sport accessory, the 'thinking person's frisbee'.

The boomerang has a well-established place in Aboriginal Dreaming stories, featuring among other transforming objects with a role in creation of the Lake Eyre region and the Flinders Ranges, for example. The boomerang's outstanding characteristic – its capacity to describe a curving trajectory or to return – is treated with matter-of-factness in these accounts. Yet it is this quality which elevated it as the Aboriginal object par excellence in the European mind, almost from its first description. As the *Dublin University Magazine* noted in 1838:

*Of all the advantages we have derived from our Australian settlements, none seems to have given more universal satisfaction than the introduction of some crooked pieces of wood shaped like the crescent moon, and called boomerang, or kilee. Ever since their structure has been fully understood, carpenters appear to have ceased from all other work;*

*the windows of toy shops display little else; walking sticks and umbrellas have gone out of fashion; and even in this rainy season no man carries anything but a boomerang; nor does this species of madness appear to be abating.*

The boomerang was more than another object used by a savage race: it seemed to overturn, or at least to arrest, laws of nature. And while this remarkable invention was quickly appropriated, the boomerang's power to arrest and bemuse has been a feature of its European history. Children of the 1960s may still recall the 'Magic Boomerang' television serial, in which a boomerang thrown by the child hero made time stand still for the duration of its flight. The same play was used by the savage urchin in the film, 'Mad Max'.

The modern history of the boomerang as the quintessential Aboriginal object has unfolded against the intermittent growth of the Aboriginal arts and craft industry. Each successive wave contributed to the remaking of Aboriginal culture in European eyes and promoted a new category of Aboriginal object. During the first of these, Aboriginal weapons were identified internationally as desirable curios, and the boomerang first achieved the popularity which it has largely retained.

The emphasis placed on Aboriginal ceremonial practice during the investigation of 'primitive religion' by British, French,

German and Australian anthropologists during the 1890s made tjurunga stones and associated ceremonial paraphernalia desirable objects for museums and private collectors. Following the National Museum of Victoria's acquisition from 1912 of a substantial collection of commissioned bark paintings, and the first Australian exhibition of primitive art in Melbourne during 1929, Arnhem Land missionaries began marketing bark paintings. A few decades later bark painting and painted Arnhem Land sculpture had all the trappings of traditional forms.

The stimulus for the creation of another category of Aboriginal art – carved and poker-worked wooden animals – was given by early tourist traffic on the East-West railway between Port Augusta and Perth, followed by the development of the Central Australian tourist industry after the Second World War. The readiness of tourists to purchase paintings which were immediately evocative of the Australian inland, rather than of Aboriginal people, coincided with a renaissance in Australian landscape art and literature. It laid the base for another Aboriginal art form which appeared to encapsulate the assimilationist ideal, that of watercolour landscape painting.

The next major development in Aboriginal art, the emergence of the Western Desert acrylic movement during the early 1970s, was also part of a wider social current. The land-rights movement, funding through the Whitlam Government, and the first indications that Australian popular culture was accommodating such notions as 'Dreaming' and 'spirit-ancestors', gave acrylic 'dot' paintings a new niche within the Australian art market.

None of these categories (apart from sacred objects) were characteristic of pre-European Aboriginal society. Despite this, each form has been interpreted and marketed as 'traditional'. Until recently, museums and galleries have sustained an illusion of primitivism and tribalism in the face of sweeping changes throughout Aboriginal society, which were set in train at the point of European contact. In 1881 the German ethnographer, Adolf Bastian, was candid enough to suggest that his own craft was, in this sense, illusory: 'For us, primitive societies [Naturvolker] are ephemeral . . . inasmuch as they exist for us all. At the very instant they become known to us they are doomed.' The media have been enthusiastic participants in sustaining the illusion, fastening particularly upon stories of tribal violence and retribution, fables of lost tribes or the 'last of the nomads'.

Today though, the last of the Pintubi has come in from the desert, and Aboriginal entrepeneurs construct sculptural totems to attract tourists. These facts have not signalled the end of the myth of primitivism. They reflect how Aboriginal art now functions outside the strict confines of tradition and tribalism. The influence of modernism in Australian art has accustomed Aboriginal art buyers to a new criterion – that of innovation itself. The opportunity to present the latest Aboriginal art, freed of reference to traditional orthodoxies or to anthropologically sanctioned definitions, has been especially welcomed by a new breed of galleries and museums attempting to fill their exhibition calendars with constant variety. Acquisition priorities, if not policies, have shifted from an imperative to fill gaps in historic collections, to capturing the range of new art styles and forms.

Against this recent phenomenon, and the entire history of Aboriginal cultural change, the boomerang has apparently survived as an unchanging icon. The boomerang's uncomplicated form has endured as a metaphor for the perceived simplicity and primitiveness of Aboriginal society and its unchanging traditions. But as Aboriginal culture becomes less easy to represent in that way, the boomerang's role also appears less certain. Its modern history has been characterised by mis-conceptions about its distribution, functions and origins. These have contributed to misunderstandings of Aboriginal culture as a whole.

Firstly, a standard assumption has been that the boomerang was used by all Aboriginal people, across the continent. This underpins the boomerang's adoption as a universal metaphor for Aborigines and for Australia. Yet the boomerang was unknown in Tasmania, by most Aboriginal people

**Daly Waters man with boomerang.** (W. Holtze, ca.1910)

of the tropical north, and by those in the western central desert regions. Like most other national stereotypes, the 'Australian Aboriginal' seems to have been created during the 1890s from an amalgam of images which had circulated in previous decades. To the silhouette of the native with spear (representing most natives of the Empire) a boomerang was added: this act of specificity also served effectively to blur the distinctions between local groups across Australia.

Secondly, the boomerang's own functions were misunderstood. There was instant confusion among early European observers as to the boomerang's capacity to kill or maim, and to return to the thrower. Returning boomerangs were used mainly in sport or in hunting wildfowl – thrown above a flock of ducks to simulate a bird of prey, the whirring boomerang would drive the birds down into nets or within range of hunters. These boomerangs, used mainly by the coastal peoples of south-eastern and south-western Australia, were light and flimsy objects, unlikely to survive a heavy impact. In contrast, the heavier and longer hunting or killing boomerangs were true weapons. They were aimed at their targets and were lethal if accurately thrown. With a degree of understatement, an early observer described the boomerang as an instrument 'thrown to disperse a crowd'. Even eyewitness accounts were distorted, to create an impression that the boomerang could create mayhem and yet return to its thrower.

The confusion between the returning boomerang and hunting or killing boomerangs was predictable. As the Aboriginal population of south-eastern Australia plummeted following exposure to European disease and the violence of the frontier, their weapons were reduced to the status of toys in the public imagination. Aboriginal people themselves appeared more like children, marginal figures in any event. As a toy, the boomerang became available for other cultures to play with. Even the concept of the boomerang became amusing, a kind of folly associated with a people who had already been a gift to cartoonists:

Q. *What do you call a boomerang that doesn't return?*

A. *A stick.*

(Christmas bon-bon joke)

The third misapprehension about the boomerang concerns its origins. Many Australians will feel cheated to learn that the boomerang was not exclusively an Aboriginal invention. Recent evidence like the 1987 find of a boomerang-like object fashioned from a mammoth tusk in southern Poland, dated to 23,000 years ago, points to that conclusion. Other prehistoric boomerangs have been discovered in Europe, although the 1974 discovery at Wyrie Swamp in South Australia still represents the world's earliest evidence (8–10,000 years) of wooden boomerangs.

Following its European discovery several theorists attempted to give the boomerang an Egyptian or even classical origin, likening it to the curved clubs of antiquity (the club of Hercules, Thor's hammer etc.). Eventually the origin most favoured was that Aboriginal people were inspired by the twisting fall of the gumleaf. After the publication of Darwin's theories, notions of independent invention rather than diffusion (usually from Ancient Egypt) were favoured by the evolutionists. The boomerang became a vital element in their argument against the degenerationists who pictured Aboriginal people as a degraded remnant of an earlier civilisation of uncertain origin. For the evolutionists, the Aboriginal invention of the boomerang proclaimed their theory's validity: if such a backward race could develop the boomerang, they were surely evolving, like every other culture, towards eventual civilisation! The boomerang became the favourite of the progressionists, ranking with the domestication of the potato and the llama by savage  migrants to the New World, and iron-working by African tribes.

From its enlistment by evolutionary theorists and practitioners, the boomerang began its long flight out of its culture of origin. Examples of the boomerang, showing its notional evolutionary progression from a simple stick, were used as the centrepieces of ethnographic exhibits in museums across the world. Boomerangs had even greater exposure in the huge International Exhibitions which followed the Great Exhibition of 1851 at London's Crystal Palace. These events were a forum for the display of manufacturing achievements and products against a backdrop of natural materials and 'savage weapons'. This juxtaposition helped confirm the lowly place of Aborigines and other hunting and gathering societies within the cultural hierarchies being established by evolutionary theory.

The International Exhibitions graphically illustrated the significance of objects in defining culture and progress. Museums were organised according to similar models, with their styles of arrangement even further elaborated through the influence of natural science classifications. The accumulating piles of boomerangs in Australia's colonial museums were incorporated with equal facility within geographical and typological arrangements.

As museum displays ossified through the following decades, these boomerang maps and schemata seemed to provide white Australians with most of what they needed to know about Aboriginal peoples. Dusty and neglected exhibitions gave apparently accurate insights into a dusty, neglected people. The rest was provided by popular culture, and here boomerangs figured even more prominently.

The 1890s were the decade in which Australians learnt to accept a large number of myths about themselves. It was also the period in which most of the symbols which were to represent the country for the next century emerged: the kangaroo image, the wattle blossom and other colonial emblems, the swagman, and the boomerang.

It was a time when the status of anthropological objects was undergoing a fundamental change. After decades of furious collecting and classification, social anthropology was beginning to replace its object-centred predecessor. As the historian Susan Bean has written:

*The differences between peoples were no longer seen to inhere in things [for example, blood and brain size, weapons and costumes]. Culture was disentangled from race. The significance of artefacts was to be found in related beliefs and social processes.* (Bean 1987: 552)

Despite its continuing role in museums, the boomerang of the 1890s was no longer confined there. Nor was it contained any longer within Aboriginal culture. It became increasingly available to popular culture, and the proliferation of advertising images which incorporated it is an indication of the enthusiasm with which the Australian public greeted the boomerang as its own. In the same way, boomerangs appeared on postcards and souvenirs made, not by Aborigines, but by Europeans. Freed to function as a 'white' object, the boomerang gained even greater potency as a military emblem and talisman. During the Second World War, the first Australian-made military aircraft was dubbed the 'Boomerang Bomber'.

Boomerangs first appeared in European homes as part of 'trophy' displays of spears and other weapons, a feature of the European frontier of the nineteenth-century Empires. As these displays went out of vogue earlier this century, they were dismantled and sold off to collectors or museums. From the 1920s onwards, new boomerang objects took their place – an astonishing range of ephemeral items which flowed into suburban houses for the following four or five decades. Aboriginal people themselves contributed to this industry; Bill Onus in Melbourne did a strong trade in boomerang tables with painted Aboriginalesque scenes.

Nevertheless, this tide of kitsch was rising against a dwindling number of Aboriginal boomerang throwers on mission stations such as Swan Reach or La Perouse.

Suddenly, in the 1990s, the tide seems to have diminished. It is difficult to locate contemporary boomerang kitsch now, even in souvenir shops. A few survivors remain, like the remarkable Boomerang Pillow, or a copper boomerang plaque ($4.95) which incorporates other Australian symbols. The boomerang image still imprints itself publicly, with the Foodland emblem in Adelaide, and its use by motels ('please return') and bus companies ('we'll bring you back home safely') across the country. But the packaged returning boomerangs sold in tourist outlets and museum shops (marked 'real' and 'authentically Australian') rarely bear any direct reference in their English and Japanese texts

Two Central Australian Aboriginal men demonstrating a boomerang fight for the photographer (probably F. Gillen) ca. 1890s.

to Aboriginal origins. These have become 'Australian' objects.

Boomerang-throwing associations have proliferated throughout the world. Nigeria has its own club; and Britain, 'The Society for the Promotion and Avoidance of Boomerangs'. Hi-tech sports boomerangs have been developed to cope with a range of bizarre new competitions ('Doubling', 'Maximum Time Aloft', etc.). An American expert specialises in having a boomerang return and cut an apple in half on his head while dressed in a William Tell outfit, a set of boomerangs representing each letter of the alphabet has been made and flown. Like 'world music', the boomerang is now available to all players, without necessary reference to its past.

Paul Hogan's chauffeur's neat appropriation of a boomerang-antennae from a New York stretch limousine in 'Crocodile Dundee' probably did as much to remind Australians of a fading image as it did to reinforce international stereotypes of this country's foibles. This revealing vignette also supplied a tidy example of the way in which Western culture has taken charge of the boomerang's flight. While some Australians feel wronged on behalf of Aboriginal people for the way in which the booomerang was removed from their culture, most are unaware that the boomerang has already flown from our shores. With all this appropriation going on, one thinks nostalgically of the Aboriginal inventor, David Unaipon, who once maintained that he had been inspired by the boomerang to invent the helicopter.

Today the most inventive and exciting aspects of Aboriginal material culture arise from the ground that lies between Aboriginal and European society. In the first decades of contact, this ground coincided with the actual frontier – it was as likely to be characterised by exploitation and atrocity as by cultural expression and exchange. During this period, moreover, Aboriginal artistic expression was mediated almost exclusively by anthropologists and collectors, rather than by popular culture. Today the anthropologists, who were always tourists of sorts, have been joined by the tourists themselves, *en masse*. Seeking to be reminded of places, cultures and times which they may, or may not, have visited, tourists have shaped and reshaped Aboriginal art and artefact markets. Their voracious demand is predicated not only on an ultimately vain quest for cultural authenticity, but on the understanding that cultural symbols can be converted into commercial possibilities. Accepting this, the souvenir and the ethnographic object become as interchangeable as their collectors, the tourist and the anthropologist:

*... tourist art is both an object with market value and a symbolic unit. It is a medium through which diverse cultures come into contact with each other and are transmitted and preserved [disturbed and distorted?]. For the tourist, every object of interest constitutes a sign of cultural practices* (Jules-Rosette 1984: 3).

Aboriginal people have responded in different ways to this demand over the last century. From the 1890s until well after the Second World War the boomerang itself, combining apparent simplicity with a suggestion of savagery, fulfilled most of the expectations which popular culture had created of Aborigines. And yet its force as a more generalised symbol, in combination with its specific properties as a confounding technological object, have placed the boomerang outside an exclusively Aboriginal context. The continuing demand for tourist art has helped to promote a range of different, innovative art and craft forms, such as the acrylic art of the Western Desert, or a recent spate of figurative carving from the same region. These new forms may rely on the tourist art industry for their initial impetus but, in contrast to the example of the boomerang itself, Aboriginal artists today are no longer constrained to continue replicating a single form delineated by Australian popular culture.

The proliferation of styles among the Western Desert painters indicate that other factors are at work. Aboriginal artists have clearly developed aesthetic and commercial standards that are both triggered by, and independent of, consumer response. And also, while the boomerang may have flown out of Aboriginal culture, Aboriginal artists have gained the autonomy to produce a growing range of new art. It is unlikely that these new art forms will remain subject to the same criteria of authenticity which were applied to the boomerang by that elite of cultural brokers – anthropologists.

# Boomerang Bibliography

## SUGGESTED READING

Davidson, D.S. 1936. 'Australian throwing sticks, throwing clubs and boomerangs'. *American Anthropologist*, 38: 76-100.

Darnell, Eric, & Ruhe, Benjamin 1985. *Boomerang: How to Throw, Catch and Make It*. New York; Workman Publishing.

Hawes, L. L. 1975. *All about Boomerangs*. Sydney: Hamlyn Group.

Hess, Felix 1975. *Boomerangs: Aerodynamics and Motion*. Gronigen, the Netherlands; privately published.

Luebbers, R.A. 1974. 'Ancient boomerangs discovered in South Australia'. *Nature*. 253: 39.

McCarthy, F.D. 1961. 'The boomerang'. *The Australian Museum Magazine*. September: 343-49.

Pahlow, P. and Silady, S. 1986. *The Complete Australian Boomerang Book*. Sydney: Alimast.

Peter, Hanns 1986. *Wesen und Bedeutung des Bumerangs*. Vienna: Wilhelm Braumuller.

Porquet, Jean-Luc & Pouillet, Dominque 1987. *Boomerang: Le Guide Complet*. Bourges: Editions Hoebeke.

Ruhe, B. 1982. *Boomerang*. Washington D.C.: Minner Press.

Ruhe, B., Darnell, E. and Morris, C. 1986. *The Boomerang Book - How to Throw, Catch and Make Them*. London: Angus & Robertson.

Thomas, Jacques 1985. *Magie du Boomerang*. Lyon: Tixier & Fils.

Weber, Klaus 1977. *Der Bumerang - Ein Rotationsflugkorper*. Frankfurt: ALS-Verlag.

## EXTENDED BIBLIOGRAPHY

Aepli, B. 1988. *Bumerang*. Zell: ZKM.

Anderson, J.C. and Jones, P.G. 1992. *Boomerang*. Adelaide: South Australian Museum.

Angas, G.F. 1847. *South Australia Illustrated*. London: Thomas McLean.

Baker, H. 1890. 'The Blackfellow and his Boomerang'. *Scribner's Magazine*. 7: 374-377.

Balfour, H. 1901. 'A swan-neck boomerang, of unusual form'. *Man*. 27.

Bates, D. 1985. *The Native Tribes of Western Australia*. Edited by Isobel White. Canberra: National Library of Australia.

Bean, S. 1987. 'The objects of anthropology'. *American Ethnologist*. 14(3): 552-559.

Blackman, L.G. 1921. 'Australian Aboriginal weapons and warfare'. *Mid-Pacific Magazine*. 21: 155-157.

Blackman, L.G. 1928. 'Weapons of the Aborigines of Australia'. *Mid-Pacific Magazine* 36: 167-172.

Bolam, A.G. 1927. *The Trans-Australian Wonderland* . Melbourne: McCubbin James.

Bradley, J.H. 1990. *Boomerangs: Complete*. Stoney Creek, Ontario: Canadian Boomerang Association.

Bretfeld, W. 1985. *Das Bumerang Buch*. Stuttgart: Franckh.

Carenvall, L. n.d. *Bumerangboken - En Handbok for den Nyfikne*. Gothenburg: The author.

Cassidy, J. 1985. *The Boomerang Book*. Palo Alto: Klute Press.

Cozzolino, M. 1980. *Symbols of Australia*. Ringwood: Penguin Books.

Clement, E. 1903. 'Ethnographical notes on the Western Australian Aborigines, with a descriptive catalogue of a collection of ethnographical objects from Western Australia by J.D.E. Schmeltz'. *Internationales Archives fur Ethnographie*. 16: 1-29.

Cleveland Boomerang School. 1989. *The Big, Small Stick Book*. Cleveland Boomerang School.

Davidson, D.S. 1936. 'Decoration of Boomerangs in Australian Aboriginal Decorative Art', *Memoirs of the American Philosophical Society*. 9: 18-28.

Davidson, D.S. 1935. 'Is the Boomerang Oriental?' *Journal of the American Oriental Society*. 55: 63-181.

Davidson, D.S. 1936. 'Australian Throwing-Sticks, Throwing-Clubs, and Boomerangs', *American Anthropologist*, 38: 76-100.

Dawson, J. 1881. *The Australian Aborigines*. Facsimile edition: Melbourne. AIATSIS.

Denton, S. T. 1889. *Incidents of a Collector's Rambles in Australia*. Boston.

Dixon, R. 1991. *Words of Our Country*. St Lucia: University of Queensland Press.

Eddy, H.J. 1882. 'On the Mechanical Principles Involved in the Flight of the Boomerang', *Proceedings of the American Association for the Advancement of Science*. 30: 22.

Eggers, H. 1888. 'A Study of the Boomerang', *Proceedings of the United States National Museum*, 363-367.

Emerson, C. H. 1893. 'Fact and Fallacy in the Boomerang Problem', *Annals of the New York Academy of Science*. 12: 77-92.

Etheridge, R. 1894. 'Three Highly Ornate Boomerangs from Bulloo River', *Proceedings of the Linnaean Society of New South Wales*. 9: 193-200.

Etheridge, R. 1896. 'Further Highly Ornate Boomerangs from New South Wales and Queensland'. *Proceedings of the Linnaean Society of New South Wales*. 21: 14-22.

Etheridge, R. 1897. 'Two Ornate Boomerangs from North Queensland', *Proceedings of the Linnaean Society of New South Wales*. 22: 260-262.

Etheridge, R. 1899. 'Further Carved Boomerangs, and two Varieties of the Langeel from Northern Queensland', *Proceedings of the Linnaean Society of New South Wales*. 23: 701-704.

Ferguson, S 1846. 'Antiquity of the Boomerang', *Tasmanian Journal of Natural Science*. 2: 238.

Fitzroy, R. 1853. 'On the Application of Steam to Ships of War'. A Paper read at the United States Institution, 18 May 1853. London.

Fox, C. 1839. 'Some notice of the Kilee or Boomerang, a Weapon Used by the Natives of Australia', *American Journal of Science*. 36: 164.

Ford, F.B.C. 1912. 'Leaf boomerang of the Belyand tribe'. *Queensland Geographical Journal*. 26: 116-121.

Fujino, A., Hawes, L.L. and Ruhe, B. 1982. *The Boomerang*. Seattle: The Pacific Museum of Flight.

Furch, A. n.d. *Theorie, fabrication, et coriemert des boomerangs*. Paris.

Gorny, W. and Schlegel, J. 1989. *Das Bumerang Projekt*. Hamburg: The authors.

Grey, G. 1841. *Journals of Two Expeditions of Discovery in North-West and Western Australia During the Years 1837-38, and 1839*. 2 vols. London: Borges & Co.

Grey, J. E. 1852. 'The Bomerang', *Philosophical Magazine*. 4: 79.

Guiart, J. 1948-1949. 'Les boomerangs d'Australie', *Revue de Geographie Humaine et d'Ethnographie*. 4: 25-34.

Gunson, N. (ed.) 1974. *Australian Reminiscences and Papers of L.E. Threlkeld*. 2 vols. Canberra: Australian Institute of Aboriginal Studies.

Hanson, M.J. 1974. *The Boomerang Book*. Harmondsworth: Puffin.

Hartman, T. 1990. *Bumerangs: Bauen, Werfen, Fangen*. Weisbaden: Englisch Verlag.

Hawes, L.L. and Mauro, J. 1975. *All about Boomerangs*. Runaway Bay: Hawes Boomerangs.

Hawes, L.L. and Ruhe, B.P. 1970. *The Boomerang*. Washington D.C.: Smithsonian Institution.

Henderson, J. and Dobson, V. (comp.) 1994. *Eastern and Central Arrernte to English Dictionary*. Alice Springs: IAD Press.

Hercus, L. and Sutton, P. (eds.) 1986. *This is What Happened*. Canberra: AIATSIS.

Hess, F. 1968. 'The aerodynamics of boomerangs'. *Scientific American*. November: 124-136.

Higgins, H.H. 1875. 'The Boomerang', *Nature*. 13: 168.

Hillyer, V. M.. 1909. 'The Boomerang in Peace and War: How to Throw It Successfully', *Life* (Melbourne): March 1909: 256-259, 312.

Horne, G. and Aiston, G. 1924. *Savage Life in Central Australia*. London: MacMillan.

Homell, J. 1924. 'South Indian Blowguns, Boomerangs, and Cross-Bow'. *Journal of the Anthropological Institute* 54: 316-346.

Howitt, A.W. 1876. 'Boomerang'. *Nature*. 14: 248-250; 15: 312.

Jennings, J. and Hardy, N H. 1899. 'On the boomerang'. *Wide World*, II: 626-629.

Jones, P.G. and Sutton, P. 1986. *Art and Land. Aboriginal Sculptures of the Lake Eyre Region*. Adelaide: South Australian Museum.

Jules-Rosette, B. 1984 *The Messages of Tourist Art: An African Semiotic System in Comparative Perspective*. New York: Plenum Press.

Krause, F. 1902. 'On throwing weapons'. *International Archives for Ethnography*. 15.

Kroeber, A.L. 1925. 'Handbook of the Indians of California'. *Bureau of American Ethnology Bulletin*. 78.

Lane-Fox (later Pitt Rivers), A. 1875. 'The Evolution of Culture'. *Journal of Proceedings of the Royal Anthropological Institute*. 7: 496-520.

Lang, F.C.A. 1911. 'Die Australischen Bumerangs in Stadtischen Volkermuseum'. *Veroffentlichen aus dem Stadischen Volkermuseum Frankfurt-am-Main*. Frankfurt-am-Main. 3.

Leak-Chevisch, P. 1949. 'The Origin of the Returning Boomerang'. *Man*. 23.

Lovering, J. 1859. 'On the Australian Weapon called the Boomerang', *Proceedings of the American Association for the Advancement of Science*. 45-63.

McCarthy, F.D. 1957. 'The Boomerang'. *Australian Museum Leaflet*. Sydney: No. 48.

Mason, B.S. 1974. *Boomerangs: How to Make and Throw Them*. New York: Dover Publications.

Mauro, J.B. 1983. *An introduction to boomerangs*. U.S. Boomerang Association.

Mayhew, H.L. 1982. *The Big Book of Boomerangs*. Columbus, Ohio: Comeback Press.

Mayhew, H.L. 1983. *How to Catch a Flying Boomerang without Using a Net*. Columbus, Ohio: Comeback Press.

Mayhew, H.L. 1987. *Boomerang Grab Bag*. Columbus, Ohio: Comeback Press.

Meggitt, M. 1962. *Desert People*. Sydney: Angus and Robertson.

Mitchell, T.L. 1852. 'Origin, History, and Description of the Boomerang Propellor'. *Athenaeum*

Mountford, C.P. and Edwards, R. 1964. 'Rock engravings in the Red Gorge, Deception Creek, Northern South Australia'. *Anthropos*. 59: 849-859

Nicols, A, 1877. 'The Boomerang', *Nature*. 15: 510

Nies, James, B. 1914. 'The Boomerang in Ancient Babylonia', *American Anthropologist*. 16: 26-32.

Noetling, F. 1911. 'Notes on the Hunting Sticks . . . of the Tasmanian Aborigines', *Papers and Proceedings of the Royal Society of Tasmania*. 63: 64-98.

'On the Boomerang', 1914. *American Anthropologist* 16.

Onus, W. 1946. 'Boomerang Magic Really Is Flying Bomb Science', *Talk* I. 42-43.

Owen, Richard. 1874. 'Contributions to the Ethnology of Egypt', *Journal of the Anthropological Institute*. 4: 223-254.

Oxley, A.E. 1939. 'Aboriginal Boomerangs Were Based on Concepts Recently Discovered', *Scientific American*. 161 190-191.

Parry, C.C. 1872. 'On a Form of the Boomerang in Use Among the Mogul Pueblo Indians of North America', *Proceedings of the American Association for the Advancement of Science*. 20: 397-400.

Payne-Gallwey, R. 1908. 'The Boomerang and How to Throw It', *Scientific American Supplement*, June 27.

Pern, S. 1928. 'Australian Boomerangs and Their Flight', *Victorian Naturalist*. 44 (4): 99-103.

Petrie, F. 1917. *British School of Archaeology in Egypt*. London.

Pignone, Giacomo Augusto 1979. *Boomerang: Fascino di un arma Preistorica*. Firenze: Editoriale Olimpia.

Pitt Rivers, A.L.F. 1872 Address, British Association, on boomerangs. *Nature*. 6: 146.

Pitt Rivers, A.L.F. 1883. 'On the Egyptian Boomerang and Its Affinities', *Journal of the Anthropological Institute*. 12: 454-463.

Porqut, J-L, and Pouillet D. 1987. *Boomerang: Le Guide Complet*. Bourges: Editions Hoebeke.

Porteus, S. 1931. *Psychology of a Primitive People*. London.

Ray, C. 1906. 'Boomerangs and Boomerang-Throwing', *Strand Magazine* 31: 87-90.

Roth, W. 1897. *Ethnological Studies among the North-West Central Queensland Aborigines*. Brisbane: Queensland Government Printer.

Ruhe, B. 1977. *Many Happy Returns: The Art and Sport of Boomeranging*. New York: Viking Press.

Rivers, W.H.R. 1915. 'The Boomerang in the New Hebrides', *Man*. 59.

Robson, D. 1977. *Why Boomerangs Return*. Baltimore: The author.

Salet, P. 1903. 'Le boomerang', *Nature*. Paris: 31: 186.

Sarg, F.C.A. 1911. 'Die Australischen bumerangs in Stadtischen Volkermuseum'. *Veroffentlichungen aus dem Stadischen Volkermuseum Frankfurt-am-Main*. Frankfurt-am-Main.

Schmeltz, J.D.E. 1888. 'On A Boomerang Ornamented with Incised Drawings of Animals', *Internationales Archives fur Ethnographie*. 1: 108-109.

Schurink, G. 1982. *Bumerangs*. Stuttgart: Franckh'sche Verlagschandlung.

Scott, F. 1907. 'The Boomerang, the Bunyip, and the Coal-Sack', *Macmillan Magazine*. 931-941.

Siems, M. 1987. *Die Bumerang Mappe*. Weinheim: Kutschera Industrie-druck.

Siems, M. 1996. *The Ultimate Boomerang Book*. Portland: D. DuFresne.

Smith, H.A. 1975. *Boomerangs: Making and Throwing Them*. Littlehampton: Gemstar Publications.

Smith, K.V. 1992. *King Bungaree. A Sydney Aborigine Meets the Great South Pacific Explorers, 1799-1830*. Kenthurst: Kangaroo Press.

Smith, W.R. 1930. *Myths and Legends of the Australian Aboriginals*. London: George Harrap & Co.

Spencer, W.B. and Gillen, F.J. 1927. *The Arunta. A Study of a Stone Age People*. London, Macmillan.

Stocker, E.O., and Tindale, N.B. 1932. 'Mt. Liebig, Reel 3 (Manufacture of weapons – boomerangs and spearthrower, also chipping of stone implements)', 400ft. 16mm film, Anthropology Archives: South Australian Museum.

Sutton, H. 1912. 'The Boomerang: The Problems of its Peculiar Flight'. *Lone Hand*, 10: 217-225.

Sutton, H. 1939. 'The Boomerang', *Mankind*, 2(7): 222-223.

Tate, R. 1880. 'South Australian Native Wooden Weapons, with Circular Incised Ornament'. *Journal of the Royal Society of South Australia*. 3: xxiii.

Thomas, J. 1991. *The Boomerangs of a Pharaoh*. Lyon: J. Thomas.

Thomas, N.W. 'Boomerangs', *Encylopaedia Britannica*. 11th edition.

Thomson, D.F. 1956. 'Exploding the Myths of Smoke Signal and Boomerang', *Melbourne Age*, April 21, 1956.

Thomson, D.F. 1957. 'Watercraft of the Australian Aborigines', *Walkabout*. 23 (June 1957): 19-20.

Thorpe, W.W. 1926. 'The Australian Boomerang', *Mid-Pacific Magazine*. 31 (March 1926): 249-255.

Thorpe, W.W. 1924. 'Boomerangs', *Australian Museum Magazine*. 2 (April 1924): 55-58.

Tindale, N.B. 1974. *Aboriginal Tribes of Australia* Berkeley:, UCLA Press.

Tunbridge, D. 1988. *Flinders Ranges Dreaming*. Canberra: Aboriginal Studies Press.

Turck, A. 1972 (1957). *Theorie fabrication et lancement des boomerangs*. Paris: Editions Chiron.

Urban, W. 1966. *Gehemnisvoller Bumerang*. Leuterhausen.

Van Gooch, L. 1942. 'Record of an Aboriginal Shield Listed as Tasmanian and a Boomerang Found Near East Devonport, Tasmania', *Records of the Queen Victoria Museum.*, 21-26.

Veit, G. 1983. *Bumerangs, Werfen Fangen und Selberbauen*. Munich: Hugendubel.

Waite, E.R. 1930. 'The Australian Boomerang. The Two types of Throwing Sticks used by the Natives of the Island Continent. The Rarity of the Returning Boomerangs and a Report of How This Unusual Weapon is Sometimes Used', *Natural History*. 30: 435-437.

Walker, G. T. 1879. 'The Boomerang', *Annual Report of the Smithsonian Institution*. 266: 1901, 515.

Walker, G.T. 1897; 1901. 'Boomerangs', *Nature*, 56: 45, 79; 64: 338-340.

Walker, G.T. 1898 'On Boomerangs', *Transactions of the Royal Society of London*. 190.

Warlukurlangu Artists. 1992. *Kuruwarri. Yuendumu Doors*. Canberra: Aboriginal Studies Press.

Weber, K. 1977. *Der Bumerang - Ein rotationsflugkorper*. Frankfurt: ALS-Verlag.

Wilkinson, 1838. 'Description of the Boomerang', in Jarman, *Voyage of the Japan, 1838*, 146-148.